C-294     **CAREER EXAMINATION SERIES**

*This is your*
*PASSBOOK for...*

# Bus Dispatcher

*Test Preparation Study Guide*
*Questions & Answers*

# COPYRIGHT NOTICE

This book is SOLELY intended for, is sold ONLY to, and its use is RESTRICTED to individual, bona fide applicants or candidates who qualify by virtue of having seriously filed applications for appropriate license, certificate, professional and/or promotional advancement, higher school matriculation, scholarship, or other legitimate requirements of education and/or governmental authorities.

This book is NOT intended for use, class instruction, tutoring, training, duplication, copying, reprinting, excerption, or adaptation, etc., by:

1) Other publishers
2) Proprietors and/or Instructors of "Coaching" and/or Preparatory Courses
3) Personnel and/or Training Divisions of commercial, industrial, and governmental organizations
4) Schools, colleges, or universities and/or their departments and staffs, including teachers and other personnel
5) Testing Agencies or Bureaus
6) Study groups which seek by the purchase of a single volume to copy and/or duplicate and/or adapt this material for use by the group as a whole without having purchased individual volumes for each of the members of the group
7) Et al.

Such persons would be in violation of appropriate Federal and State statutes.

PROVISION OF LICENSING AGREEMENTS – Recognized educational, commercial, industrial, and governmental institutions and organizations, and others legitimately engaged in educational pursuits, including training, testing, and measurement activities, may address request for a licensing agreement to the copyright owners, who will determine whether, and under what conditions, including fees and charges, the materials in this book may be used them.  In other words, a licensing facility exists for the legitimate use of the material in this book on other than an individual basis.  However, it is asseverated and affirmed here that the material in this book CANNOT be used without the receipt of the express permission of such a licensing agreement from the Publishers. Inquiries re licensing should be addressed to the company, attention rights and permissions department.

All rights reserved, including the right of reproduction in whole or in part, in any form or by any means, electronic or mechanical, including photocopying, recording, or by any information storage and retrieval system, without permission in writing from the Publisher.

Copyright © 2024 by
## National Learning Corporation

212 Michael Drive, Syosset, NY 11791
(516) 921-8888 • www.passbooks.com
E-mail: info@passbooks.com

PUBLISHED IN THE UNITED STATES OF AMERICA

# PASSBOOK® SERIES

THE *PASSBOOK® SERIES* has been created to prepare applicants and candidates for the ultimate academic battlefield – the examination room.

At some time in our lives, each and every one of us may be required to take an examination – for validation, matriculation, admission, qualification, registration, certification, or licensure.

Based on the assumption that every applicant or candidate has met the basic formal educational standards, has taken the required number of courses, and read the necessary texts, the *PASSBOOK® SERIES* furnishes the one special preparation which may assure passing with confidence, instead of failing with insecurity. Examination questions – together with answers – are furnished as the basic vehicle for study so that the mysteries of the examination and its compounding difficulties may be eliminated or diminished by a sure method.

This book is meant to help you pass your examination provided that you qualify and are serious in your objective.

The entire field is reviewed through the huge store of content information which is succinctly presented through a provocative and challenging approach – the question-and-answer method.

A climate of success is established by furnishing the correct answers at the end of each test.

You soon learn to recognize types of questions, forms of questions, and patterns of questioning. You may even begin to anticipate expected outcomes.

You perceive that many questions are repeated or adapted so that you can gain acute insights, which may enable you to score many sure points.

You learn how to confront new questions, or types of questions, and to attack them confidently and work out the correct answers.

You note objectives and emphases, and recognize pitfalls and dangers, so that you may make positive educational adjustments.

Moreover, you are kept fully informed in relation to new concepts, methods, practices, and directions in the field.

You discover that you are actually taking the examination all the time: you are preparing for the examination by "taking" an examination, not by reading extraneous and/or supererogatory textbooks.

In short, this PASSBOOK®, used directedly, should be an important factor in helping you to pass your test.

# BUS DISPATCHER

## DUTIES
Dispatchers assign bus operators to their runs; direct the dispatch and movement of buses within an assigned territory; handle unusual occurrences in service; determine ways to minimize delays incidental to bus operations; make computations relative to bus schedules; investigate accidents, unusual occurrences and equipment failures; keep time records; prepare reports; and communicate via radio. When required, Dispatchers operate Bus Company vehicles on the road or in the yards; and perform related work.

## SCOPE OF THE EXAMINATION
The multiple-choice test may include questions on rules, regulations and procedures governing the timely, safe and efficient operation of buses; supervision of bus operators and related personnel, including the assignment of bus operators to bus runs; computations related to bus schedules; procedures in the event of accidents, crimes, illnesses or other unusual occurrences; record-keeping procedures and forms commonly used by dispatchers; and other related areas.

# HOW TO TAKE A TEST

I. YOU MUST PASS AN EXAMINATION

## A. WHAT EVERY CANDIDATE SHOULD KNOW

Examination applicants often ask us for help in preparing for the written test. What can I study in advance? What kinds of questions will be asked? How will the test be given? How will the papers be graded?

As an applicant for a civil service examination, you may be wondering about some of these things. Our purpose here is to suggest effective methods of advance study and to describe civil service examinations.

Your chances for success on this examination can be increased if you know how to prepare. Those "pre-examination jitters" can be reduced if you know what to expect. You can even experience an adventure in good citizenship if you know why civil service exams are given.

## B. WHY ARE CIVIL SERVICE EXAMINATIONS GIVEN?

Civil service examinations are important to you in two ways. As a citizen, you want public jobs filled by employees who know how to do their work. As a job seeker, you want a fair chance to compete for that job on an equal footing with other candidates. The best-known means of accomplishing this two-fold goal is the competitive examination.

Exams are widely publicized throughout the nation. They may be administered for jobs in federal, state, city, municipal, town or village governments or agencies.

Any citizen may apply, with some limitations, such as the age or residence of applicants. Your experience and education may be reviewed to see whether you meet the requirements for the particular examination. When these requirements exist, they are reasonable and applied consistently to all applicants. Thus, a competitive examination may cause you some uneasiness now, but it is your privilege and safeguard.

## C. HOW ARE CIVIL SERVICE EXAMS DEVELOPED?

Examinations are carefully written by trained technicians who are specialists in the field known as "psychological measurement," in consultation with recognized authorities in the field of work that the test will cover. These experts recommend the subject matter areas or skills to be tested; only those knowledges or skills important to your success on the job are included. The most reliable books and source materials available are used as references. Together, the experts and technicians judge the difficulty level of the questions.

Test technicians know how to phrase questions so that the problem is clearly stated. Their ethics do not permit "trick" or "catch" questions. Questions may have been tried out on sample groups, or subjected to statistical analysis, to determine their usefulness.

Written tests are often used in combination with performance tests, ratings of training and experience, and oral interviews. All of these measures combine to form the best-known means of finding the right person for the right job.

## II. HOW TO PASS THE WRITTEN TEST

### A. NATURE OF THE EXAMINATION

To prepare intelligently for civil service examinations, you should know how they differ from school examinations you have taken. In school you were assigned certain definite pages to read or subjects to cover. The examination questions were quite detailed and usually emphasized memory. Civil service exams, on the other hand, try to discover your present ability to perform the duties of a position, plus your potentiality to learn these duties. In other words, a civil service exam attempts to predict how successful you will be. Questions cover such a broad area that they cannot be as minute and detailed as school exam questions.

In the public service similar kinds of work, or positions, are grouped together in one "class." This process is known as *position-classification*. All the positions in a class are paid according to the salary range for that class. One class title covers all of these positions, and they are all tested by the same examination.

### B. FOUR BASIC STEPS

#### 1) Study the announcement

How, then, can you know what subjects to study? Our best answer is: "Learn as much as possible about the class of positions for which you've applied." The exam will test the knowledge, skills and abilities needed to do the work.

Your most valuable source of information about the position you want is the official exam announcement. This announcement lists the training and experience qualifications. Check these standards and apply only if you come reasonably close to meeting them.

The brief description of the position in the examination announcement offers some clues to the subjects which will be tested. Think about the job itself. Review the duties in your mind. Can you perform them, or are there some in which you are rusty? Fill in the blank spots in your preparation.

Many jurisdictions preview the written test in the exam announcement by including a section called "Knowledge and Abilities Required," "Scope of the Examination," or some similar heading. Here you will find out specifically what fields will be tested.

#### 2) Review your own background

Once you learn in general what the position is all about, and what you need to know to do the work, ask yourself which subjects you already know fairly well and which need improvement. You may wonder whether to concentrate on improving your strong areas or on building some background in your fields of weakness. When the announcement has specified "some knowledge" or "considerable knowledge," or has used adjectives like "beginning principles of…" or "advanced … methods," you can get a clue as to the number and difficulty of questions to be asked in any given field. More questions, and hence broader coverage, would be included for those subjects which are more important in the work. Now weigh your strengths and weaknesses against the job requirements and prepare accordingly.

#### 3) Determine the level of the position

Another way to tell how intensively you should prepare is to understand the level of the job for which you are applying. Is it the entering level? In other words, is this the position in which beginners in a field of work are hired? Or is it an intermediate or advanced level? Sometimes this is indicated by such words as "Junior" or "Senior" in the class title. Other jurisdictions use Roman numerals to designate the level – Clerk I, Clerk II, for example. The word "Supervisor" sometimes appears in the title. If the level is not indicated by the title, check the description of duties. Will you be working under very close supervision, or will you have responsibility for independent decisions in this work?

### 4) Choose appropriate study materials

Now that you know the subjects to be examined and the relative amount of each subject to be covered, you can choose suitable study materials. For beginning level jobs, or even advanced ones, if you have a pronounced weakness in some aspect of your training, read a modern, standard textbook in that field. Be sure it is up to date and has general coverage. Such books are normally available at your library, and the librarian will be glad to help you locate one. For entry-level positions, questions of appropriate difficulty are chosen – neither highly advanced questions, nor those too simple. Such questions require careful thought but not advanced training.

If the position for which you are applying is technical or advanced, you will read more advanced, specialized material. If you are already familiar with the basic principles of your field, elementary textbooks would waste your time. Concentrate on advanced textbooks and technical periodicals. Think through the concepts and review difficult problems in your field.

These are all general sources. You can get more ideas on your own initiative, following these leads. For example, training manuals and publications of the government agency which employs workers in your field can be useful, particularly for technical and professional positions. A letter or visit to the government department involved may result in more specific study suggestions, and certainly will provide you with a more definite idea of the exact nature of the position you are seeking.


## III. KINDS OF TESTS

Tests are used for purposes other than measuring knowledge and ability to perform specified duties. For some positions, it is equally important to test ability to make adjustments to new situations or to profit from training. In others, basic mental abilities not dependent on information are essential. Questions which test these things may not appear as pertinent to the duties of the position as those which test for knowledge and information. Yet they are often highly important parts of a fair examination. For very general questions, it is almost impossible to help you direct your study efforts. What we can do is to point out some of the more common of these general abilities needed in public service positions and describe some typical questions.

1) General information

Broad, general information has been found useful for predicting job success in some kinds of work. This is tested in a variety of ways, from vocabulary lists to questions about current events. Basic background in some field of work, such as sociology or economics, may be sampled in a group of questions. Often these are principles which have become familiar to most persons through exposure rather than through formal training. It is difficult to advise you how to study for these questions; being alert to the world around you is our best suggestion.

2) Verbal ability

An example of an ability needed in many positions is verbal or language ability. Verbal ability is, in brief, the ability to use and understand words. Vocabulary and grammar tests are typical measures of this ability. Reading comprehension or paragraph interpretation questions are common in many kinds of civil service tests. You are given a paragraph of written material and asked to find its central meaning.

3) Numerical ability

Number skills can be tested by the familiar arithmetic problem, by checking paired lists of numbers to see which are alike and which are different, or by interpreting charts and graphs. In the latter test, a graph may be printed in the test booklet which you are asked to use as the basis for answering questions.

4) Observation

A popular test for law-enforcement positions is the observation test. A picture is shown to you for several minutes, then taken away. Questions about the picture test your ability to observe both details and larger elements.

5) Following directions

In many positions in the public service, the employee must be able to carry out written instructions dependably and accurately. You may be given a chart with several columns, each column listing a variety of information. The questions require you to carry out directions involving the information given in the chart.

6) Skills and aptitudes

Performance tests effectively measure some manual skills and aptitudes. When the skill is one in which you are trained, such as typing or shorthand, you can practice. These tests are often very much like those given in business school or high school courses. For many of the other skills and aptitudes, however, no short-time preparation can be made. Skills and abilities natural to you or that you have developed throughout your lifetime are being tested.

Many of the general questions just described provide all the data needed to answer the questions and ask you to use your reasoning ability to find the answers. Your best preparation for these tests, as well as for tests of facts and ideas, is to be at your physical and mental best. You, no doubt, have your own methods of getting into an exam-taking mood and keeping "in shape." The next section lists some ideas on this subject.


IV. KINDS OF QUESTIONS

Only rarely is the "essay" question, which you answer in narrative form, used in civil service tests. Civil service tests are usually of the short-answer type. Full instructions for answering these questions will be given to you at the examination. But in case this is your first experience with short-answer questions and separate answer sheets, here is what you need to know:

1) **Multiple-choice Questions**

Most popular of the short-answer questions is the "multiple choice" or "best answer" question. It can be used, for example, to test for factual knowledge, ability to solve problems or judgment in meeting situations found at work.

A multiple-choice question is normally one of three types—
- It can begin with an incomplete statement followed by several possible endings. You are to find the one ending which *best* completes the statement, although some of the others may not be entirely wrong.
- It can also be a complete statement in the form of a question which is answered by choosing one of the statements listed.

- It can be in the form of a problem – again you select the best answer.

Here is an example of a multiple-choice question with a discussion which should give you some clues as to the method for choosing the right answer:

When an employee has a complaint about his assignment, the action which will *best* help him overcome his difficulty is to
   A. discuss his difficulty with his coworkers
   B. take the problem to the head of the organization
   C. take the problem to the person who gave him the assignment
   D. say nothing to anyone about his complaint

In answering this question, you should study each of the choices to find which is best. Consider choice "A" – Certainly an employee may discuss his complaint with fellow employees, but no change or improvement can result, and the complaint remains unresolved. Choice "B" is a poor choice since the head of the organization probably does not know what assignment you have been given, and taking your problem to him is known as "going over the head" of the supervisor. The supervisor, or person who made the assignment, is the person who can clarify it or correct any injustice. Choice "C" is, therefore, correct. To say nothing, as in choice "D," is unwise. Supervisors have and interest in knowing the problems employees are facing, and the employee is seeking a solution to his problem.

## 2) True/False Questions

The "true/false" or "right/wrong" form of question is sometimes used. Here a complete statement is given. Your job is to decide whether the statement is right or wrong.

SAMPLE: A roaming cell-phone call to a nearby city costs less than a non-roaming call to a distant city.

This statement is wrong, or false, since roaming calls are more expensive.
This is not a complete list of all possible question forms, although most of the others are variations of these common types. You will always get complete directions for answering questions. Be sure you understand *how* to mark your answers – ask questions until you do.

## V. RECORDING YOUR ANSWERS

Computer terminals are used more and more today for many different kinds of exams.
For an examination with very few applicants, you may be told to record your answers in the test booklet itself. Separate answer sheets are much more common. If this separate answer sheet is to be scored by machine – and this is often the case – it is highly important that you mark your answers correctly in order to get credit.
An electronic scoring machine is often used in civil service offices because of the speed with which papers can be scored. Machine-scored answer sheets must be marked with a pencil, which will be given to you. This pencil has a high graphite content which responds to the electronic scoring machine. As a matter of fact, stray dots may register as answers, so do not let your pencil rest on the answer sheet while you are pondering the correct answer. Also, if your pencil lead breaks or is otherwise defective, ask for another.

Since the answer sheet will be dropped in a slot in the scoring machine, be careful not to bend the corners or get the paper crumpled.

The answer sheet normally has five vertical columns of numbers, with 30 numbers to a column. These numbers correspond to the question numbers in your test booklet. After each number, going across the page are four or five pairs of dotted lines. These short dotted lines have small letters or numbers above them. The first two pairs may also have a "T" or "F" above the letters. This indicates that the first two pairs only are to be used if the questions are of the true-false type. If the questions are multiple choice, disregard the "T" and "F" and pay attention only to the small letters or numbers.

Answer your questions in the manner of the sample that follows:

32. The largest city in the United States is
 A. Washington, D.C.
 B. New York City
 C. Chicago
 D. Detroit
 E. San Francisco

1) Choose the answer you think is best. (New York City is the largest, so "B" is correct.)
2) Find the row of dotted lines numbered the same as the question you are answering. (Find row number 32)
3) Find the pair of dotted lines corresponding to the answer. (Find the pair of lines under the mark "B.")
4) Make a solid black mark between the dotted lines.


## VI. BEFORE THE TEST

Common sense will help you find procedures to follow to get ready for an examination. Too many of us, however, overlook these sensible measures. Indeed, nervousness and fatigue have been found to be the most serious reasons why applicants fail to do their best on civil service tests. Here is a list of reminders:

- Begin your preparation early – Don't wait until the last minute to go scurrying around for books and materials or to find out what the position is all about.
- Prepare continuously – An hour a night for a week is better than an all-night cram session. This has been definitely established. What is more, a night a week for a month will return better dividends than crowding your study into a shorter period of time.
- Locate the place of the exam – You have been sent a notice telling you when and where to report for the examination. If the location is in a different town or otherwise unfamiliar to you, it would be well to inquire the best route and learn something about the building.
- Relax the night before the test – Allow your mind to rest. Do not study at all that night. Plan some mild recreation or diversion; then go to bed early and get a good night's sleep.
- Get up early enough to make a leisurely trip to the place for the test – This way unforeseen events, traffic snarls, unfamiliar buildings, etc. will not upset you.
- Dress comfortably – A written test is not a fashion show. You will be known by number and not by name, so wear something comfortable.

- Leave excess paraphernalia at home – Shopping bags and odd bundles will get in your way. You need bring only the items mentioned in the official notice you received; usually everything you need is provided. Do not bring reference books to the exam. They will only confuse those last minutes and be taken away from you when in the test room.
- Arrive somewhat ahead of time – If because of transportation schedules you must get there very early, bring a newspaper or magazine to take your mind off yourself while waiting.
- Locate the examination room – When you have found the proper room, you will be directed to the seat or part of the room where you will sit. Sometimes you are given a sheet of instructions to read while you are waiting. Do not fill out any forms until you are told to do so; just read them and be prepared.
- Relax and prepare to listen to the instructions
- If you have any physical problem that may keep you from doing your best, be sure to tell the test administrator. If you are sick or in poor health, you really cannot do your best on the exam. You can come back and take the test some other time.

## VII. AT THE TEST

The day of the test is here and you have the test booklet in your hand. The temptation to get going is very strong. Caution! There is more to success than knowing the right answers. You must know how to identify your papers and understand variations in the type of short-answer question used in this particular examination. Follow these suggestions for maximum results from your efforts:

### 1) Cooperate with the monitor

The test administrator has a duty to create a situation in which you can be as much at ease as possible. He will give instructions, tell you when to begin, check to see that you are marking your answer sheet correctly, and so on. He is not there to guard you, although he will see that your competitors do not take unfair advantage. He wants to help you do your best.

### 2) Listen to all instructions

Don't jump the gun! Wait until you understand all directions. In most civil service tests you get more time than you need to answer the questions. So don't be in a hurry. Read each word of instructions until you clearly understand the meaning. Study the examples, listen to all announcements and follow directions. Ask questions if you do not understand what to do.

### 3) Identify your papers

Civil service exams are usually identified by number only. You will be assigned a number; you must not put your name on your test papers. Be sure to copy your number correctly. Since more than one exam may be given, copy your exact examination title.

### 4) Plan your time

Unless you are told that a test is a "speed" or "rate of work" test, speed itself is usually not important. Time enough to answer all the questions will be provided, but this does not mean that you have all day. An overall time limit has been set. Divide the total time (in minutes) by the number of questions to determine the approximate time you have for each question.

### 5) Do not linger over difficult questions

If you come across a difficult question, mark it with a paper clip (useful to have along) and come back to it when you have been through the booklet. One caution if you do this – be sure to skip a number on your answer sheet as well. Check often to be sure that you have not lost your place and that you are marking in the row numbered the same as the question you are answering.

### 6) Read the questions

Be sure you know what the question asks! Many capable people are unsuccessful because they failed to *read* the questions correctly.

### 7) Answer all questions

Unless you have been instructed that a penalty will be deducted for incorrect answers, it is better to guess than to omit a question.

### 8) Speed tests

It is often better NOT to guess on speed tests. It has been found that on timed tests people are tempted to spend the last few seconds before time is called in marking answers at random – without even reading them – in the hope of picking up a few extra points. To discourage this practice, the instructions may warn you that your score will be "corrected" for guessing. That is, a penalty will be applied. The incorrect answers will be deducted from the correct ones, or some other penalty formula will be used.

### 9) Review your answers

If you finish before time is called, go back to the questions you guessed or omitted to give them further thought. Review other answers if you have time.

### 10) Return your test materials

If you are ready to leave before others have finished or time is called, take ALL your materials to the monitor and leave quietly. Never take any test material with you. The monitor can discover whose papers are not complete, and taking a test booklet may be grounds for disqualification.

## VIII. EXAMINATION TECHNIQUES

1) Read the general instructions carefully. These are usually printed on the first page of the exam booklet. As a rule, these instructions refer to the timing of the examination; the fact that you should not start work until the signal and must stop work at a signal, etc. If there are any *special* instructions, such as a choice of questions to be answered, make sure that you note this instruction carefully.

2) When you are ready to start work on the examination, that is as soon as the signal has been given, read the instructions to each question booklet, underline any key words or phrases, such as *least, best, outline, describe* and the like. In this way you will tend to answer as requested rather than discover on reviewing your paper that you *listed without describing*, that you selected the *worst* choice rather than the *best* choice, etc.

3) If the examination is of the objective or multiple-choice type – that is, each question will also give a series of possible answers: A, B, C or D, and you are called upon to select the best answer and write the letter next to that answer on your answer paper – it is advisable to start answering each question in turn. There may be anywhere from 50 to 100 such questions in the three or four hours allotted and you can see how much time would be taken if you read through all the questions before beginning to answer any. Furthermore, if you come across a question or group of questions which you know would be difficult to answer, it would undoubtedly affect your handling of all the other questions.

4) If the examination is of the essay type and contains but a few questions, it is a moot point as to whether you should read all the questions before starting to answer any one. Of course, if you are given a choice – say five out of seven and the like – then it is essential to read all the questions so you can eliminate the two that are most difficult. If, however, you are asked to answer all the questions, there may be danger in trying to answer the easiest one first because you may find that you will spend too much time on it. The best technique is to answer the first question, then proceed to the second, etc.

5) Time your answers. Before the exam begins, write down the time it started, then add the time allowed for the examination and write down the time it must be completed, then divide the time available somewhat as follows:
   - If 3-1/2 hours are allowed, that would be 210 minutes. If you have 80 objective-type questions, that would be an average of 2-1/2 minutes per question. Allow yourself no more than 2 minutes per question, or a total of 160 minutes, which will permit about 50 minutes to review.
   - If for the time allotment of 210 minutes there are 7 essay questions to answer, that would average about 30 minutes a question. Give yourself only 25 minutes per question so that you have about 35 minutes to review.

6) The most important instruction is to *read each question* and make sure you know what is wanted. The second most important instruction is to *time yourself properly* so that you answer every question. The third most important instruction is to *answer every question*. Guess if you have to but include something for each question. Remember that you will receive no credit for a blank and will probably receive some credit if you write something in answer to an essay question. If you guess a letter – say "B" for a multiple-choice question – you may have guessed right. If you leave a blank as an answer to a multiple-choice question, the examiners may respect your feelings but it will not add a point to your score. Some exams may penalize you for wrong answers, so in such cases *only*, you may not want to guess unless you have some basis for your answer.

7) Suggestions
   a. Objective-type questions
      1. Examine the question booklet for proper sequence of pages and questions
      2. Read all instructions carefully
      3. Skip any question which seems too difficult; return to it after all other questions have been answered
      4. Apportion your time properly; do not spend too much time on any single question or group of questions

5. Note and underline key words – *all, most, fewest, least, best, worst, same, opposite,* etc.
6. Pay particular attention to negatives
7. Note unusual option, e.g., unduly long, short, complex, different or similar in content to the body of the question
8. Observe the use of "hedging" words – *probably, may, most likely,* etc.
9. Make sure that your answer is put next to the same number as the question
10. Do not second-guess unless you have good reason to believe the second answer is definitely more correct
11. Cross out original answer if you decide another answer is more accurate; do not erase until you are ready to hand your paper in
12. Answer all questions; guess unless instructed otherwise
13. Leave time for review

   b. Essay questions
     1. Read each question carefully
     2. Determine exactly what is wanted. Underline key words or phrases.
     3. Decide on outline or paragraph answer
     4. Include many different points and elements unless asked to develop any one or two points or elements
     5. Show impartiality by giving pros and cons unless directed to select one side only
     6. Make and write down any assumptions you find necessary to answer the questions
     7. Watch your English, grammar, punctuation and choice of words
     8. Time your answers; don't crowd material

8) Answering the essay question

Most essay questions can be answered by framing the specific response around several key words or ideas. Here are a few such key words or ideas:

M's: manpower, materials, methods, money, management
P's: purpose, program, policy, plan, procedure, practice, problems, pitfalls, personnel, public relations

   a. Six basic steps in handling problems:
     1. Preliminary plan and background development
     2. Collect information, data and facts
     3. Analyze and interpret information, data and facts
     4. Analyze and develop solutions as well as make recommendations
     5. Prepare report and sell recommendations
     6. Install recommendations and follow up effectiveness

   b. Pitfalls to avoid
     1. *Taking things for granted* – A statement of the situation does not necessarily imply that each of the elements is necessarily true; for example, a complaint may be invalid and biased so that all that can be taken for granted is that a complaint has been registered

2. *Considering only one side of a situation* – Wherever possible, indicate several alternatives and then point out the reasons you selected the best one
3. *Failing to indicate follow up* – Whenever your answer indicates action on your part, make certain that you will take proper follow-up action to see how successful your recommendations, procedures or actions turn out to be
4. *Taking too long in answering any single question* – Remember to time your answers properly

## IX. AFTER THE TEST

Scoring procedures differ in detail among civil service jurisdictions although the general principles are the same. Whether the papers are hand-scored or graded by machine we have described, they are nearly always graded by number. That is, the person who marks the paper knows only the number – never the name – of the applicant. Not until all the papers have been graded will they be matched with names. If other tests, such as training and experience or oral interview ratings have been given, scores will be combined. Different parts of the examination usually have different weights. For example, the written test might count 60 percent of the final grade, and a rating of training and experience 40 percent. In many jurisdictions, veterans will have a certain number of points added to their grades.

After the final grade has been determined, the names are placed in grade order and an eligible list is established. There are various methods for resolving ties between those who get the same final grade – probably the most common is to place first the name of the person whose application was received first. Job offers are made from the eligible list in the order the names appear on it. You will be notified of your grade and your rank as soon as all these computations have been made. This will be done as rapidly as possible.

People who are found to meet the requirements in the announcement are called "eligibles." Their names are put on a list of eligible candidates. An eligible's chances of getting a job depend on how high he stands on this list and how fast agencies are filling jobs from the list.

When a job is to be filled from a list of eligibles, the agency asks for the names of people on the list of eligibles for that job. When the civil service commission receives this request, it sends to the agency the names of the three people highest on this list. Or, if the job to be filled has specialized requirements, the office sends the agency the names of the top three persons who meet these requirements from the general list.

The appointing officer makes a choice from among the three people whose names were sent to him. If the selected person accepts the appointment, the names of the others are put back on the list to be considered for future openings.

That is the rule in hiring from all kinds of eligible lists, whether they are for typist, carpenter, chemist, or something else. For every vacancy, the appointing officer has his choice of any one of the top three eligibles on the list. This explains why the person whose name is on top of the list sometimes does not get an appointment when some of the persons lower on the list do. If the appointing officer chooses the second or third eligible, the No. 1 eligible does not get a job at once, but stays on the list until he is appointed or the list is terminated.

# X. HOW TO PASS THE INTERVIEW TEST

The examination for which you applied requires an oral interview test. You have already taken the written test and you are now being called for the interview test – the final part of the formal examination.

You may think that it is not possible to prepare for an interview test and that there are no procedures to follow during an interview. Our purpose is to point out some things you can do in advance that will help you and some good rules to follow and pitfalls to avoid while you are being interviewed.

*What is an interview supposed to test?*

The written examination is designed to test the technical knowledge and competence of the candidate; the oral is designed to evaluate intangible qualities, not readily measured otherwise, and to establish a list showing the relative fitness of each candidate – as measured against his competitors – for the position sought. Scoring is not on the basis of "right" and "wrong," but on a sliding scale of values ranging from "not passable" to "outstanding." As a matter of fact, it is possible to achieve a relatively low score without a single "incorrect" answer because of evident weakness in the qualities being measured.

Occasionally, an examination may consist entirely of an oral test – either an individual or a group oral. In such cases, information is sought concerning the technical knowledges and abilities of the candidate, since there has been no written examination for this purpose. More commonly, however, an oral test is used to supplement a written examination.

*Who conducts interviews?*

The composition of oral boards varies among different jurisdictions. In nearly all, a representative of the personnel department serves as chairman. One of the members of the board may be a representative of the department in which the candidate would work. In some cases, "outside experts" are used, and, frequently, a businessman or some other representative of the general public is asked to serve. Labor and management or other special groups may be represented. The aim is to secure the services of experts in the appropriate field.

However the board is composed, it is a good idea (and not at all improper or unethical) to ascertain in advance of the interview who the members are and what groups they represent. When you are introduced to them, you will have some idea of their backgrounds and interests, and at least you will not stutter and stammer over their names.

*What should be done before the interview?*

While knowledge about the board members is useful and takes some of the surprise element out of the interview, there is other preparation which is more substantive. It *is* possible to prepare for an oral interview – in several ways:

### 1) Keep a copy of your application and review it carefully before the interview

This may be the only document before the oral board, and the starting point of the interview. Know what education and experience you have listed there, and the sequence and dates of all of it. Sometimes the board will ask you to review the highlights of your experience for them; you should not have to hem and haw doing it.

### 2) Study the class specification and the examination announcement

Usually, the oral board has one or both of these to guide them. The qualities, characteristics or knowledges required by the position sought are stated in these documents. They offer valuable clues as to the nature of the oral interview. For example, if the job involves supervisory responsibilities, the announcement will usually indicate that knowledge of modern supervisory methods and the qualifications of the candidate as a supervisor will be tested. If so, you can expect such questions, frequently in the form of a hypothetical situation which you are expected to solve. NEVER go into an oral without knowledge of the duties and responsibilities of the job you seek.

### 3) Think through each qualification required

Try to visualize the kind of questions you would ask if you were a board member. How well could you answer them? Try especially to appraise your own knowledge and background in each area, *measured against the job sought*, and identify any areas in which you are weak. Be critical and realistic – do not flatter yourself.

### 4) Do some general reading in areas in which you feel you may be weak

For example, if the job involves supervision and your past experience has NOT, some general reading in supervisory methods and practices, particularly in the field of human relations, might be useful. Do NOT study agency procedures or detailed manuals. The oral board will be testing your understanding and capacity, not your memory.

### 5) Get a good night's sleep and watch your general health and mental attitude

You will want a clear head at the interview. Take care of a cold or any other minor ailment, and of course, no hangovers.

*What should be done on the day of the interview?*

Now comes the day of the interview itself. Give yourself plenty of time to get there. Plan to arrive somewhat ahead of the scheduled time, particularly if your appointment is in the fore part of the day. If a previous candidate fails to appear, the board might be ready for you a bit early. By early afternoon an oral board is almost invariably behind schedule if there are many candidates, and you may have to wait. Take along a book or magazine to read, or your application to review, but leave any extraneous material in the waiting room when you go in for your interview. In any event, relax and compose yourself.

The matter of dress is important. The board is forming impressions about you – from your experience, your manners, your attitude, and your appearance. Give your personal appearance careful attention. Dress your best, but not your flashiest. Choose conservative, appropriate clothing, and be sure it is immaculate. This is a business interview, and your appearance should indicate that you regard it as such. Besides, being well groomed and properly dressed will help boost your confidence.

Sooner or later, someone will call your name and escort you into the interview room. *This is it.* From here on you are on your own. It is too late for any more preparation. But remember, you asked for this opportunity to prove your fitness, and you are here because your request was granted.

*What happens when you go in?*

The usual sequence of events will be as follows: The clerk (who is often the board stenographer) will introduce you to the chairman of the oral board, who will introduce you to the other members of the board. Acknowledge the introductions before you sit down. Do not be surprised if you find a microphone facing you or a stenotypist sitting by. Oral interviews are usually recorded in the event of an appeal or other review.

Usually the chairman of the board will open the interview by reviewing the highlights of your education and work experience from your application – primarily for the benefit of the other members of the board, as well as to get the material into the record. Do not interrupt or comment unless there is an error or significant misinterpretation; if that is the case, do not hesitate. But do not quibble about insignificant matters. Also, he will usually ask you some question about your education, experience or your present job – partly to get you to start talking and to establish the interviewing "rapport." He may start the actual questioning, or turn it over to one of the other members. Frequently, each member undertakes the questioning on a particular area, one in which he is perhaps most competent, so you can expect each member to participate in the examination. Because time is limited, you may also expect some rather abrupt switches in the direction the questioning takes, so do not be upset by it. Normally, a board member will not pursue a single line of questioning unless he discovers a particular strength or weakness.

After each member has participated, the chairman will usually ask whether any member has any further questions, then will ask you if you have anything you wish to add. Unless you are expecting this question, it may floor you. Worse, it may start you off on an extended, extemporaneous speech. The board is not usually seeking more information. The question is principally to offer you a last opportunity to present further qualifications or to indicate that you have nothing to add. So, if you feel that a significant qualification or characteristic has been overlooked, it is proper to point it out in a sentence or so. Do not compliment the board on the thoroughness of their examination – they have been sketchy, and you know it. If you wish, merely say, "No thank you, I have nothing further to add." This is a point where you can "talk yourself out" of a good impression or fail to present an important bit of information. Remember, *you close the interview yourself.*

The chairman will then say, "That is all, Mr. _____, thank you." Do not be startled; the interview is over, and quicker than you think. Thank him, gather your belongings and take your leave. Save your sigh of relief for the other side of the door.

*How to put your best foot forward*

Throughout this entire process, you may feel that the board individually and collectively is trying to pierce your defenses, seek out your hidden weaknesses and embarrass and confuse you. Actually, this is not true. They are obliged to make an appraisal of your qualifications for the job you are seeking, and they want to see you in your best light. Remember, they must interview all candidates and a non-cooperative candidate may become a failure in spite of their best efforts to bring out his qualifications. Here are 15 suggestions that will help you:

**1) Be natural – Keep your attitude confident, not cocky**

If you are not confident that you can do the job, do not expect the board to be. Do not apologize for your weaknesses, try to bring out your strong points. The board is interested in a positive, not negative, presentation. Cockiness will antagonize any board member and make him wonder if you are covering up a weakness by a false show of strength.

**2) Get comfortable, but don't lounge or sprawl**

Sit erectly but not stiffly. A careless posture may lead the board to conclude that you are careless in other things, or at least that you are not impressed by the importance of the occasion. Either conclusion is natural, even if incorrect. Do not fuss with your clothing, a pencil or an ashtray. Your hands may occasionally be useful to emphasize a point; do not let them become a point of distraction.

**3) Do not wisecrack or make small talk**

This is a serious situation, and your attitude should show that you consider it as such. Further, the time of the board is limited – they do not want to waste it, and neither should you.

### 4) Do not exaggerate your experience or abilities

In the first place, from information in the application or other interviews and sources, the board may know more about you than you think. Secondly, you probably will not get away with it. An experienced board is rather adept at spotting such a situation, so do not take the chance.

### 5) If you know a board member, do not make a point of it, yet do not hide it

Certainly you are not fooling him, and probably not the other members of the board. Do not try to take advantage of your acquaintanceship – it will probably do you little good.

### 6) Do not dominate the interview

Let the board do that. They will give you the clues – do not assume that you have to do all the talking. Realize that the board has a number of questions to ask you, and do not try to take up all the interview time by showing off your extensive knowledge of the answer to the first one.

### 7) Be attentive

You only have 20 minutes or so, and you should keep your attention at its sharpest throughout. When a member is addressing a problem or question to you, give him your undivided attention. Address your reply principally to him, but do not exclude the other board members.

### 8) Do not interrupt

A board member may be stating a problem for you to analyze. He will ask you a question when the time comes. Let him state the problem, and wait for the question.

### 9) Make sure you understand the question

Do not try to answer until you are sure what the question is. If it is not clear, restate it in your own words or ask the board member to clarify it for you. However, do not haggle about minor elements.

### 10) Reply promptly but not hastily

A common entry on oral board rating sheets is "candidate responded readily," or "candidate hesitated in replies." Respond as promptly and quickly as you can, but do not jump to a hasty, ill-considered answer.

### 11) Do not be peremptory in your answers

A brief answer is proper – but do not fire your answer back. That is a losing game from your point of view. The board member can probably ask questions much faster than you can answer them.

### 12) Do not try to create the answer you think the board member wants

He is interested in what kind of mind you have and how it works – not in playing games. Furthermore, he can usually spot this practice and will actually grade you down on it.

### 13) Do not switch sides in your reply merely to agree with a board member

Frequently, a member will take a contrary position merely to draw you out and to see if you are willing and able to defend your point of view. Do not start a debate, yet do not surrender a good position. If a position is worth taking, it is worth defending.

**14) Do not be afraid to admit an error in judgment if you are shown to be wrong**

The board knows that you are forced to reply without any opportunity for careful consideration. Your answer may be demonstrably wrong. If so, admit it and get on with the interview.

**15) Do not dwell at length on your present job**

The opening question may relate to your present assignment. Answer the question but do not go into an extended discussion. You are being examined for a *new* job, not your present one. As a matter of fact, try to phrase ALL your answers in terms of the job for which you are being examined.

*Basis of Rating*

Probably you will forget most of these "do's" and "don'ts" when you walk into the oral interview room. Even remembering them all will not ensure you a passing grade. Perhaps you did not have the qualifications in the first place. But remembering them will help you to put your best foot forward, without treading on the toes of the board members.

Rumor and popular opinion to the contrary notwithstanding, an oral board wants you to make the best appearance possible. They know you are under pressure – but they also want to see how you respond to it as a guide to what your reaction would be under the pressures of the job you seek. They will be influenced by the degree of poise you display, the personal traits you show and the manner in which you respond.

ABOUT THIS BOOK

This book contains tests divided into Examination Sections. Go through each test, answering every question in the margin. We have also attached a sample answer sheet at the back of the book that can be removed and used. At the end of each test look at the answer key and check your answers. On the ones you got wrong, look at the right answer choice and learn. Do not fill in the answers first. Do not memorize the questions and answers, but understand the answer and principles involved. On your test, the questions will likely be different from the samples. Questions are changed and new ones added. If you understand these past questions you should have success with any changes that arise. Tests may consist of several types of questions. We have additional books on each subject should more study be advisable or necessary for you. Finally, the more you study, the better prepared you will be. This book is intended to be the last thing you study before you walk into the examination room. Prior study of relevant texts is also recommended. NLC publishes some of these in our Fundamental Series. Knowledge and good sense are important factors in passing your exam. Good luck also helps. So now study this Passbook, absorb the material contained within and take that knowledge into the examination. Then do your best to pass that exam.

# EXAMINATION SECTION

# EXAMINATION SECTION
# TEST 1

DIRECTIONS: Each question or incomplete statement is followed by several suggested answers or completions. Select the one that BEST answers the question or completes the statement. *PRINT THE LETTER OF THE CORRECT ANSWER IN THE SPACE AT THE RIGHT.*

1. Assume that you are appointed a dispatcher and that an angry passenger gets off a bus and complains to you about poor bus service in general.
   Your BEST procedure to follow, from among the following, is to

   A. listen and avoid commenting
   B. tell the passenger to use other means of transportation
   C. suggest to the passenger that he is wrong
   D. walk away, since the passenger is unreasonable

   1.____

2. In performing his job, it is LEAST important for a road dispatcher to

   A. know the bus routes in his area very well
   B. know the bus operators on his line very well
   C. make sure buses are kept on schedule
   D. be able to handle accident situations

   2.____

3. The dispatcher who is USUALLY responsible for posting bulletin orders on the bulletin board of a depot is the

   A. crew dispatcher
   B. general dispatcher
   C. the P.M. senior surface line dispatcher
   D. the location chief

   3.____

4. If you suspect a reporting operator to be under the influence of alcohol, the PROPER action to be taken is to

   A. smell his breath and have him walk a straight line to test his sobriety
   B. confiscate his badge and pass, and tell him he is suspended
   C. have him fill out a sick report, and send him home
   D. direct him to submit to a blood-alcohol examination

   4.____

5. The LEAST effective procedure, from among the following, for overcoming carelessness on the part of a bus operator is to

   A. strictly administer discipline when necessary
   B. supervise him closely
   C. give him less difficult assignments
   D. make sure he is trained thoroughly

   5.____

6. Depending upon the amount of damage involved, the state vehicle and traffic laws require a person operating a motor vehicle to report an accident involving property damage to the commissioner of motor vehicles.
   A report does NOT have to be filed when the amount of the damage is

   6.____

1

A. $150 and it involves the property of a person other than the driver causing the accident
B. more than $200 and it involves the property of a person other than the driver causing the accident
C. $275 and it involves only the property of the driver causing the accident
D. $250 and no one was injured

7. With respect to the 2-way radio system, Code 2 is used in reporting a situation where a

   A. passenger has fallen in a bus and has injured himself
   B. bus has become disabled
   C. bus has collided with another vehicle
   D. bus is blocked by fire apparatus

8. When an employee changes his address, he must notify the authority within

   A. 48 hours    B. 4 days    C. 1 week    D. 2 weeks

9. Employees may engage in card playing while on system property

   A. at no time
   B. only during a lunch period
   C. before or after their working hours
   D. when not actively performing their duties

10. A passenger can request the name and pass or badge number of an employee who is in contact with the public.
    If this happens, the employee MUST provide the requested information to the passenger

    A. if the passenger insists strenuously
    B. if the passenger provides a valid reason
    C. without delay or argument
    D. without argument after first trying to pacify and reason with the passenger

11. Assume that a total of 345 people are employed at a certain location.
    If 2/5 of these people report to work at 7:00 A.M. and another 1/5 at 8:00 A.M., then the number of people that have NOT yet reported to work is closest to

    A. 73    B. 138    C. 154    D. 199

12. When an operator is involved in an accident enroute and he reports it over the 2-way radio, the operator is next required to give a verbal report of this accident to the

    A. first dispatcher he personally contacts
    B. general dispatcher at the depot
    C. crew dispatcher at the depot
    D. location chief after he has pulled in to his depot

13. The total number of depots operated directly by the authority is

    A. 5    B. 8    C. 9    D. 10

14. If a fuel storage tank contains 11,200 gallons of fuel when it is 85% full, its MAXIMUM capacity, in gallons, is closest to

    A. 9,589  B. 13,175  C. 13,274  D. 14,107

15. If an unloaded pistol is found on authority property, it MUST be

    A. forwarded to the lost property office by special messenger
    B. turned over to the office of the assistant superintendent of the division
    C. forwarded to the operations center at a designated bus depot by special messenger
    D. turned over to the transit police

16. Assume that a bus consumes an average of 8 gallons of fuel per hour and that each gallon of fuel weighs 7 1/2 pounds.
    In a 6-hour period, the amount of fuel used, in pounds, is CLOSEST to

    A. 108  B. 232  C. 348  D. 399

17. The agency of the government that regulates the use of the 2-way radio system is the

    A. Federal Communication Commission
    B. Public Service Commission
    C. Interstate Commerce Commission
    D. The Bureau of Radio Regulation

18. For the two-way radio system, Code 12 is used for

    A. hold-up attempts
    B. a disabled bus
    C. certain winter operations
    D. bomb threat situations

19. Since operators no longer provide cash change for passengers, the rule that operators are held accountable for the collection of bus fares

    A. has been officially dropped
    B. must still be strictly adhered to
    C. cannot be adhered to
    D. is no longer important

20. When a passenger claims to have been involved in an accident on a bus and wishes information about filing a claim, you should tell him

    A. that a representative of the authority will communicate with him
    B. that you are not allowed to make any statements
    C. to contact the authority's law department
    D. to see his own lawyer before making a statement

21. The reason which would be of MOST benefit to the authority for investigating an accident is

   A. that it is a requirement of the accident prevention committee
   B. to determine the extent of bus damage and any property damage
   C. to obtain knowledge that will prevent future accidents
   D. to determine the extent of injuries to either employees or the public

22. Surface line operators are required to examine bulletin boards

   A. whenever it seems necessary
   B. before going on duty
   C. before going off duty
   D. at least once each week

23. The authority sick leave year begins on _____ 1st.

   A. January     B. May     C. April     D. December

24. From 8:00 A.M. to 11:00 A.M. on a particular bus line, the one way running time in each direction is 38 minutes, while the headway time is 8 minutes and the layover time at each terminal is 6 minutes.
   The number of buses that are required during this time period is CLOSEST to

   A. 6     B. 9     C. 10     D. 11

25. The assumption that accidents USUALLY result from carelessness

   A. is generally correct
   B. does not apply in the case of employees with many years of experience
   C. does not apply in the case of employees who are closely supervised
   D. should never be made

26. Some bulletin orders are reissued periodically. Generally, the MAIN purpose for doing this is to

   A. clarify rules that are not clear
   B. keep operators alert to important rules and notices
   C. make sure these bulletin orders are posted on all bulletin boards
   D. replace old bulletin orders having obsolete information

27. An A.M. transfer bearing the date of May 4 and having its P.M. coupon detached is NOT valid

   A. from 11:00 P.M., May 3, until 1:00 P.M., May 4
   B. on May 4 from 12:01 A.M. until 2:00 P.M.
   C. on May 4 from 12:01 A.M. until 1:00 P.M.
   D. from 11:00 P.M., May 3, until 12:00 Noon, May 4

28. On a particular bus line, 4 buses per hour are scheduled to leave a terminal between the hours of 5:00 A.M. and 7:00 A.M., while 6 buses per hour are scheduled to leave between 7:00 A.M. and 9:00 A.M.
   The reduction in headway after 7:00 A.M. is CLOSEST to _____ minutes.

   A. 5     B. 10     C. 15     D. 20

Questions 29-40.

DIRECTIONS: Questions 29 through 40 are based on the sample schedule shown below. Refer to this schedule when answering these questions. Assume that all operations proceed as scheduled unless otherwise stated in the question.

ROUTES: S-10-OXFORD AVENUE     KING DEPOT
WEEKDAY SCHEDULE NO. SL-53
EFFECTIVE:    2/8

**HEADWAYS**
From Alice St. and from Hall St.

| Time | Min. |
|---|---|
| 12:00 Mid. | - |
| 5:00 AM | 15 Min. |
| 6:30 AM | 10 |
| 9:00 AM | 6 |
| 2:00 PM | 10 |
| 6:30 PM | 6 |
| 12:00 Mid. | 10 |

**RUNNING TIME**
From Alice St. and from Hall St.

| | 1:00 AM – 6:30 AM | 6:30 AM – 1:00 AM |
|---|---|---|
| Alice St. | - | - |
| Bean St. | 4 | 6 |
| Charles St. | 6 | 7 |
| Doon St. | 6 | 9 |
| Ellen St. | 4 | 6 |
| Frank St. | 5 | 8 |
| Gem St. | 5 | 7 |
| Hall St. | 6 | 7 |
| Totals | 36 | 50 |

PASSENGER ROUTE MILES PER TRIP = 6.6 MILES
RUN ON/RUN OFF MILES BETWEEN KING DEPOT AND ALICE ST. = 1.4 MILES
SOUTHBOUND BUSES LEAVE FROM ALICE ST.
NORTHBOUND BUSES LEAVE FROM HALL ST.

29. The bus leaving Alice Street at 7:12 A.M. should arrive at Hall Street _____ minutes later.

    A. 36     B. 42     C. 50     D. 56

30. The bus leaving Alice Street at 6:20 A.M. should arrive at Ellen Street at _____ A.M.

    A. 6:38     B. 6:40     C. 6:42     D. 6:45

31. The buses leaving Alice Street at 6:20 A.M. and 6:30 A.M. should arrive at Hall Street _____ minutes apart.

    A. 10     B. 13     C. 15     D. 17

32. The southbound bus leaving Charles Street at 6:20 A.M. should arrive at Gem Street at _____ A.M.

    A. 6:40     B. 6:42     C. 6:45     D. 6:52

33. If the southbound bus leaving Alice Street at 6:30 A.M. is delayed for 6 minutes at Doon Street and takes 5 minutes longer than scheduled to run from Doon Street to Ellen Street, this bus will arrive at Hall Street at approximately _____ A.M.

    A. 7:31     B. 7:34     C. 7:36     D. 7:40

34. Between 6:00 A.M. and 8:00 A.M., there should be a southbound bus leaving Alice Street at

    A. 6:40　　　B. 7:02　　　C. 7:06　　　D. 7:56

35. The bus leaving Alice Street at 6:10 A.M. should arrive at Hall Street at _____ A.M.

    A. 6:46　　　B. 6:52　　　C. 6:57　　　D. 7:00

36. A southbound bus that reaches Frank Street at 6:53 A.M. would MOST likely be

    A. 4 minutes early　　　B. 10 minutes early
    C. 3 minutes late　　　　D. on time

37. The average speed for a bus traveling from Alice Street to Hall Street between the hours of 2:00 A.M. and 4:00 A.M. is CLOSEST to _____ mph.

    A. 7　　　B. 9　　　C. 11　　　D. 13

38. Assuming a recovery time of 8 minutes at the Hall Street terminal, a bus leaving Alice Street at 6:10 A.M. should arrive back at Alice Street at APPROXIMATELY _____ A.M.

    A. 7:30　　　B. 7:44　　　C. 7:50　　　D. 7:58

39. The total number of southbound buses that should be traveling enroute between terminals from 6:30 A.M. to 6:59 A.M. is CLOSEST to

    A. 5　　　B. 6　　　C. 7　　　D. 8

40. Between 6:00 A.M. and 9:00 A.M., there should be a southbound bus arriving at Hall Street at

    A. 6:36　　　B. 7:20　　　C. 8:04　　　D. 8:30

---

# KEY (CORRECT ANSWERS)

| | | | | | | | |
|---|---|---|---|---|---|---|---|
| 1. | A | 11. | B | 21. | C | 31. | B |
| 2. | B | 12. | A | 22. | B | 32. | C |
| 3. | B | 13. | D | 23. | B | 33. | A |
| 4. | D | 14. | B | 24. | D | 34. | C |
| 5. | C | 15. | D | 25. | A | 35. | B |
| 6. | A | 16. | C | 26. | B | 36. | D |
| 7. | A | 17. | A | 27. | B | 37. | C |
| 8. | C | 18. | D | 28. | A | 38. | C |
| 9. | A | 19. | B | 29. | C | 39. | D |
| 10. | C | 20. | C | 30. | D | 40. | B |

# TEST 2

DIRECTIONS: Each question or incomplete statement is followed by several suggested answers or completions. Select the one that BEST answers the question or completes the statement. *PRINT THE LETTER OF THE CORRECT ANSWER IN THE SPACE AT THE RIGHT.*

1. When a general dispatcher assigns a code responsibility classification of *D* for an accident, it indicates that the operator was _____ at fault.

    A. 25%  B. 50%  C. 75%  D. 100%

    1._____

2. A road dispatcher sees a bus traveling and it is emitting fumes.
   Although the bus is NOT on a route belonging to him, he should report this bus by calling

    A. surface control
    B. the air pollution control board
    C. the yard dispatcher
    D. the location chief

    2._____

3. Assume that you are appointed a dispatcher and that an unusual emergency occurs involving authority operations and you have NO time to contact a superior.
   From among the following, the BEST procedure to follow is to

    A. discuss the situation with all the people involved in the emergency
    B. take no action unless you are forced to
    C. attempt to consult with another dispatcher
    D. take immediate action according to your best judgment

    3._____

4. Assume that you are appointed a dispatcher and that a member of the special inspection department shows you his identification card and asks you a question.
   You should

    A. tell him to see your supervisor
    B. try to answer his question
    C. call your supervisor first before answering his question
    D. ask him for more identification

    4._____

5. The regular equipment of every bus includes a fire extinguisher.
   To operate the fire extinguisher, it is necessary to first

    A. press the lever and then pull the safety pin
    B. pull the safety pin and then press the lever
    C. make sure the safety pin has not been pulled and then press the lever
    D. break the safety pin and then push the lever

    5._____

6. The opening fare reading on a daily register card is 1152 and the last fare reading is 1463; the opening cash reading is 12015 and the last cash closing reading is 24345.
   The total number of revenue paying passengers that this bus carried on this day is CLOSEST to

    A. 722  B. 1,112  C. 1,463  D. 12,330

    6._____

7. On the surface bus condition report, if an operator marked an X in the box for NO DEFROST, the trouble would be shown on this report under the category

    A. A.C. & HEAT
    B. MISCELLANEOUS
    C. WINDOWS
    D. ELECTRICAL

8. When a bus is turned short of its scheduled destination, the operator should enter on the daily trip report the code letter

    A. A    B. B    C. C    D. D

9. When a bus operator has made certain that it is safe to back up, he must signal by tooting his horn

    A. once
    B. twice
    C. three times
    D. four times

10. An employee was assigned to emergency work after completion of his regularly scheduled tour of duty.
    Since the employee worked 13 hours of emergency work, he will be paid _____ meal allowance(s).

    A. 1    B. 2    C. 3    D. 4

11. A bus operator with a weekday run pulls out of the depot at 9:54 A.M., swings from 2:23 P.M. to 3:13 P.M., and is relieved at a relied point at 5:05 P.M. The travel allowance back to the depot is 16 minutes, and the headway allowance for this run is 20 minutes. Including all allowances, the pay for this run, in hours and minutes, is CLOSEST to

    A. 8:00    B. 8:07    C. 8:20    D. 8:30

12. If an operator is required to prepare an accident report after his regular clearing time, he will be given a report-writing allowance of

    A. 1 hour minus any boost time
    B. 1 hour
    C. 1 hour minus 1/2 any boost time
    D. 1/2 hour

13. Under normal conditions, operators of buses on streets used by only one bus line must keep a spacing distance between moving buses of NOT less than _____ feet.

    A. 10    B. 50    C. 100    D. 150

14. Of the following, it is MOST reasonable to expect that a bus operator who practices *defensive driving* will

    A. not have accidents
    B. be able to prevent most accidents
    C. be a good surface line dispatcher
    D. never be legally at fault in an accident

15. It is MOST likely that operators will perform their jobs more willingly and effectively if dispatchers

    A. overlook the majority of minor violations
    B. show some favoritism

C. are liberal in granting overtime
D. utilize good judgment in their supervision

16. In general, it is GOOD practice to

    A. race a bus engine to build up air pressure
    B. idle a bus engine when the oil pressure becomes low
    C. operate the bus with at least 50 pounds of air pressure
    D. stop the bus engine when it becomes overheated

17. The BEST method for an operator to use in order to learn about new rules is to

    A. read all bulletins when they are issued
    B. refer to the book of rules and regulations
    C. question the crew and general dispatchers
    D. consult with other operators

18. A bus line has 50 regular runs.
    The MINIMUM number of regular runs that must be open on this line before a pick is required to be held is

    A. 2   B. 4   C. 5   D. 10

19. From among the following reasons, the BEST reason for requiring an operator to make out an accident report as soon as possible after an accident is that

    A. the operator will still remember the important details accurately
    B. responsibility for the accident must be determined within 24 hours
    C. this will provide the authority with more time to investigate the accident
    D. the report can then be kept confidential more easily

20. When the location chief is absent at a depot, the dispatcher who USUALLY acts for him is the _____ dispatcher.

    A. crew              B. general
    C. depot control     D. chief surface line

21. Camber, caster, and toe-in are terms that apply PRIMARILY to the

    A. lubrication system of an engine
    B. front-end alignment
    C. brake system
    D. transmission

22. An employee, who is home during a snow emergency, has been ordered to telephone his depot.
    If the employee calls once and he is NOT ordered to report for snow emergency work, he will be allowed

    A. nothing
    B. 1/2 hours pay at his regular rate
    C. 1 hours pay at his regular rate
    D. 1 hour and 30 minutes pay at his regular rate

4 (#2)

23. An operator has a run which reports on Saturday at 11:41 A.M., swings from 4:49 P.M. until 5:29 P.M., and clears at 7:47 P.M.
    The night differential for this run, in hours and minutes, is CLOSEST to

    A.  1:47      B.  7:26      C.  8:06      D.  8:09

24. An operator who returns to work after a two-day absence due to illness must submit a sick application within _____ day(s) after his return to work.

    A.  1         B.  2         C.  3         D.  4

25. A regular operator off sick during a change in pick will be paid on the basis of _____ pay.

    A.  his new run            B.  his old run
    C.  division              D.  60% sick

26. If an incident involving radioactive material occurs, it is necessary to immediately notify the

    A.  superintendent of operations
    B.  location chief
    C.  division chief
    D.  transit police

27. Of the following, it is MOST important to the public to have buses that

    A.  are very comfortable
    B.  are capable of traveling at high speed
    C.  have low fuel consumption
    D.  do not break down frequently

Questions 28-40.

DIRECTIONS:   Questions 28 through 40 are based on the partly filled in schedule shown on the next page. Use this schedule in answering Questions 28 through 40.

USE THIS SCHEDULE FOR ANSWERING QUESTIONS 28 TO 40.

DIVISION: MONTGOMERY
DEPOT: VICTORIA
LINE OF ROUTE: B-409 CLIFF ST.

IN EFFECT: 1-1        Week Day
Schedule No. 1 604

| | | | TIME - HOURS & MINUTES | | | | | |
|---|---|---|---|---|---|---|---|---|
| | | | | | PAY TIME | | | |
| TRIPS | SPREAD | SWING | TRAVEL | VEHICLE | ALLOWANCE | SWING | MILEAGE DIFF. | TOTAL PAY |

| Run | Report | | | | | | | | | | | Mileage | Clear |
|---|---|---|---|---|---|---|---|---|---|---|---|---|---|
| 3 | AM 450 | P.O. 500 | Y 511 | 521 606 | 701 746 | 837 929 | - 951 | 1041 1109 R-5 | 1109 1208 | - 1234 R-8 | | 48 18 | 100 |
| 4 | 510 | P.O. 520 | Y 531 | 541 626 | 717 806 | 853 945 | 1046 - | 1143 R-8 | - 1219 R-14 | R.O. 108 127 | P.I. | 57 18 | .137 |
| 5 | 530 | P.O. 540 | Y 551 | 601 646 | 733 826 | 925 1015 | - 1041 | 1119 R-7 | 1153 1249 | 116 115 R-19 | | 48 18 | 141 |
| 10 | 925 | R-3 | 951 - | 1025 1121 | 1147 1204 | R-6 - | - 125 | 1223 1253 R-9 | 245 340 R-15 | 437 525 228 | 558 517 | | 18 49 33 | 624 33 606 |
| 11 | 941 | P.O. 951 | Y 1002 | 1013 1107 | 1259 | R-18 | 1109 R-14 | R-3 | 156 - | 325 420 | 540 R-23 | | | |
| 27 | PM 458 | R-18 524 | - 556 | - 612 | 653 748 | R.O. 837 845 | P.I. 856 | 1223 R-26 | 954 R-3 | - 1024 | 1122 1215 | 1236 R-32 | 33 25 | 102 |
| 28 | 514 | R-11 540 | | | 709 804 | 902 955 | - 1021 | R-26 | 1116 R-30 | 1149 1241 | - | R.O. 122 129 | P.I. 140 | 40 26 | 150 |

SYMBOLS
PLAIN TRIPS - Apple St. and Beaver St. to Pear St. and Wolf St.
Y TRIPS - Cliff St. and Hill St. to Apple St. and Beaver St.
RO TRIPS - Apple St. and Beaver St. to Cliff St. and Hill St., thence to Depot.
P.O. - Pull Out        P.I. - Pull In

NOTES
FROM: Apple St. and Beaver St. - Via Apple St., Cliff St., Pear St. to Wolf St.
RETURN: Via Pear St., Cliff St., Apple St. to Beaver St.

RELIEFS MADE AT ORANGE ST. AND PEAR ST., 16 MINUTE TRAVEL ALLOWANCE - VIA ROUTE Y-502

6 (#2)

28. The total travel allowance for Run No. 27, in minutes, is CLOSEST to  28._____
    A. 16  B. 32  C. 48  D. 56

29. The paid swing for Run No. 27, in minutes, is CLOSEST to  29._____
    A. 0  B. 32  C. 42  D. 58

30. The total pay for Run No. 3, in hours and minutes, is CLOSEST to  30._____
    A. 8:00  B. 8:10  C. 8:15  D. 8:31

31. The vehicle time for Run No. 28, in hours and minutes, is CLOSEST to  31._____
    A. 6:54  B. 7:05  C. 7:21  D. 7:41

32. From among the following runs, the one which has the LEAST travel allowance is Run No.  32._____
    A. 3  B. 4  C. 5  D. 10

33. The spread for Run No. 5, in hours and minutes, is CLOSEST to  33._____
    A. 7:25  B. 8:00  C. 8:11  D. 8:31

34. For Run No. 3, the total number of trips, including any to and from the depot, for the first half of the run is  34._____
    A. 7  B. 8  C. 9  D. 10

35. The total pay for Run No. 11, in hours and minutes, is CLOSEST to  35._____
    A. 8:00  B. 8:25  C. 8:31  D. 8:38

36. The operator on Run No. 5 should get  36._____
    A. an overtime allowance of 6 minutes
    B. an overtime allowance of 11 minutes
    C. a boost allowance of 27 minutes
    D. no boost or overtime allowance

37. The overtime allowance for Run No. 28, in minutes, is CLOSEST to  37._____
    A. 0  B. 18  C. 36  D. 54

38. From among the following runs, the one which pays the LEAST night differential is Run No.  38._____
    A. 3  B. 4  C. 5  D. 10

39. The total travel allowance for Run No. 28, in minutes, is CLOSEST to  39._____
    A. 0  B. 16  C. 32  D. 48

40. The operator who has the MOST run-on and run-off trips is the operator on Run No.  40._____
    A. 4  B. 5  C. 10  D. 27

## KEY (CORRECT ANSWERS)

| | | | |
|---|---|---|---|
| 1. C | 11. C | 21. B | 31. B |
| 2. A | 12. A | 22. D | 32. B |
| 3. D | 13. C | 23. C | 33. C |
| 4. B | 14. B | 24. C | 34. B |
| 5. B | 15. D | 25. B | 35. B |
| 6. A | 16. D | 26. D | 36. D |
| 7. A | 17. A | 27. D | 37. A |
| 8. B | 18. C | 28. C | 38. D |
| 9. C | 19. A | 29. C | 39. B |
| 10. C | 20. B | 30. B | 40. A |

# EXAMINATION SECTION
# TEST 1

DIRECTIONS: Each question or incomplete statement is followed by several suggested answers or completions. Select the one that BEST answers the question or completes the statement. *PRINT THE LETTER OF THE CORRECT ANSWER IN THE SPACE AT THE RIGHT.*

1. As a dispatcher, you note that there have been an excessive number of *Runs Not Out* for the past week.
   Your FIRST action should be to

   A. refer the facts to special inspection
   B. report this to surface control
   C. investigate the cause
   D. enlarge the extra list

2. One traffic lane on many wide one-way streets is marked out in yellow paint.
   This lane is to be

   A. cleared for vehicles about to make a left turn
   B. used exclusively by emergency vehicles
   C. used by regular vehicles when a siren is heard
   D. cleared for emergency vehicles when a siren is heard

3. The number of feet required to bring a bus traveling at 30 MPH to a stop at a braking rate of 3 miles per hour per second is NEAREST to _____ feet.

   A. 180        B. 200        C. 220        D. 240

4. Improper use of the horn of a motor vehicle is not permitted.
   It would be CLEARLY improper for a bus operator to sound

   A. two short blasts as he is passing another bus going in the opposite direction
   B. three short blasts as a warning before he backs up
   C. several short blasts to warn a motorist about to pull away from the curb in front of his moving bus
   D. several short blasts to warn pedestrian stragglers in front of his bus at an intersection

5. A dispatcher desires to check the speed of a certain 40-foot bus.
   If he times the bus as passing him in 1.5 seconds, then the bus is traveling at APPROXIMATELY _____ MPH.

   A. 15        B. 18        C. 22        D. 27

6. A safety report for a recent month shows there were 5,368 employees, 950,127 man-hours of exposure, and 16 accidents in surface transportation, whereas in surface maintenance there were 1,486 employees, 238,617 man-hours of exposure, and 19 accidents.
   From these figures, it can be concluded that

   A. the accident rate was much lower in maintenance than in transportation
   B. maintenance work is about 20% more hazardous than bus operation

C. the average transportation employee put in 10% more time than the average maintenance employee
D. there are more transportation employees than are needed

7. With respect to operators' runs or tricks, it is TRUE that 7.____

   A. a paid lunch period is allowed for swing runs with more than 6 hours work before the swing
   B. 75% of all regular runs must be completed within a spread of ten hours
   C. time-and-one-half is paid for swing run time in excess of ten hours
   D. 65% of the total number of regular runs must be straight runs

8. A depot pick is MOST likely to be held whenever 8.____

   A. a line is transferred from one depot to another
   B. runs are added to or eliminated from the schedule
   C. 10% of the regular runs (at least 2 runs) on a line are open
   D. the regular schedule for a line out of that depot is changed

9. If two operators wish to permanently exchange runs after a pick has been completed, the HIGHEST official approval required is that of the 9.____

   A. general dispatcher
   B. crew dispatcher
   C. location chief
   D. assistant general superintendent

10. A recognized principle in good urban transportation is that the headway at any particular time of day should be uniform. 10.____
    The consequence of an irregular headway resulting from traffic conditions is MOST likely to be

    A. confusion of passengers
    B. heavy riding on some buses
    C. loss of patronage
    D. crossing accidents

11. According to regulations, an operator who is called to take a civil service promotion examination at 9 A.M. on Saturday need NOT be excused from any part of his tour if the tour 11.____

    A. *ends* after 1 A.M. Saturday
    B. *begins* between 8 and 10 P.M. Friday
    C. *ends* between 9 and 11 A.M. Saturday
    D. *begins* between 3 and 4 P.M. Saturday

12. The regulation against picking up or discharging passengers at other than designated bus stops is a requirement of the 12.____

    A. Department of Licenses     B. Police Department
    C. Department of Traffic      D. Department of Highways

13. Five minutes after making a relief at a location away from the depot, the relieving operator is involved in a collision with a truck and is found to have alcoholic breath. In this case, it is MANDATORY to take disciplinary action against the offending operator and the

    A. patrol dispatcher
    B. operator he relieved
    C. location chief
    D. general dispatcher

13._____

14. A failure which does NOT necessarily require that a bus be taken out of service is _____ door stuck _____.

    A. front; closed
    B. front; open
    C. rear; closed
    D. rear; open

14._____

15. An operator calls surface control to report that a passenger in his bus has had a heart attack.
    The operator should be instructed to

    A. stay where he is until the sick passenger has been removed in an ambulance
    B. drive to the nearest hospital emergency entrance and have the passenger removed
    C. stay where he is until the sick passenger is removed by road dispatchers in a patrol car
    D. get other passengers to help place the sick passenger in a taxicab and have the passenger taken to a hospital

15._____

16. At depots, accident records are kept in _____ order.

    A. chronological
    B. alphabetical
    C. pass number
    D. badge number

16._____

17. Eighty percent of the 300 operators in your depot are married, and 50% of all operators are under 35 years of age.
    The MINIMUM number of married operators in this lower age group is

    A. 60    B. 90    C. 150    D. 240

17._____

18. If an operator submits a claim that his place on the depot seniority list is incorrect and the time of submission of the claim is within 5 days of the time the list was posted, he is entitled to an answer from the location chief within _____ day(s).

    A. 1    B. 2    C. 5    D. 10

18._____

19. Dual rear tires are used on buses PRIMARILY to

    A. increase traction
    B. avoid blowouts
    C. distribute vehicle weight
    D. overcome friction

19._____

20. A bus maintained a speed of 5 MPH for one-third of its route, 10 MPH for the second third, and 15 MPH for the final third.
    The AVERAGE speed for the entire route was CLOSEST to _____ MPH.

    A. 8    B. 9    C. 10    D. 11

20._____

21. The terminal-to-terminal running time on a bus route is 42 minutes, and there is a ten-minute layover at each terminal.
Allowing 10% for stopping and breakdowns, the MINIMUM number of buses required to maintain a 5-minute headway in both directions on this route is nearest to

    A. 11   B. 12   C. 21   D. 23

22. Items of information which would NOT ordinarily be found in the depot log are

    A. names of employees on the extra list
    B. notations of rerouting of buses
    C. special instructions
    D. notations of formal employee grievances received

23. A dispatcher received a controversial order and while verbally transmitting it to his subordinates briefly justified the controversial parts.
This procedure was

    A. *incorrect,* because the dispatcher need not explain any order to his subordinates
    B. *correct,* because most subordinates would otherwise not comply with the controversial parts
    C. *correct,* because a few explanatory remarks on an order of this kind may well eliminate complaints
    D. *incorrect,* because this action might draw attention to the controversial parts which might otherwise have been overlooked

24. When a certain operator reports for duty, the dispatcher informs him that he must take a specific detour because of some construction work. The operator informs the dispatcher that he knows that part of the proposed detour is also closed to traffic.
In this case, it would be BEST for the dispatcher to

    A. insist that the operator take the detour he was given
    B. radio a road dispatcher and order him to the obstructed location to lay out a usable detour
    C. tell the operator to take any usable detour at the obstructed location and report when he gets back to the depot
    D. immediately bring this doubtful matter to the attention of higher authority

25. After an operator uses a bus fire extinguisher, he must make a notation on the bus maintenance record and

    A. notify the location chief
    B. notify central dispatch
    C. submit an accident report
    D. make an entry in the depot log

26. In deciding whether to take disciplinary action against an operator, it would be LEAST valuable for a dispatcher to know

    A. when to refer the matter to higher authority
    B. when the matter requires immediate action
    C. the employment record of the man since joining the transit system
    D. the employment record of the man prior to joining the transit system

27. It is an indication of a safe driver if the operator  27._____

    A. *frequently* yields the right-of-way
    B. *seldom* runs ahead of schedule
    C. *frequently* runs behind schedule
    D. *seldom* yields the right-of-way

28. If a dispatcher finds a mistake in the details of a bulletin order recently issued to operators, the BEST procedure for him to follow would be to  28._____

    A. call the error to the attention of higher authority
    B. expect the operators to notice the error in the details of the order and take the correct action
    C. ask the other dispatchers to explain the order to the operators and correct it
    D. issue a new bulletin order superseding and correcting the original order

29. A personal acquaintance who knows your official position has had his civic association send you a personal invitation to speak to them at a meeting about bus transportation and to answer questions from the floor.
    You would be using the POOREST judgment if your answer to the civic association was that  29._____

    A. you were too busy and had no time to spend with them
    B. they should send a formal request for a speaker to the transit authority
    C. you would check with higher authority before accepting or declining this opportunity
    D. you would accept without reservations this opportunity to speak to them

30. A man asks your permission to take motion pictures in the depot which you supervise. Your PROPER action is to  30._____

    A. deny the request because regulations forbid picture taking on transit authority property
    B. grant the request if he signs a waiver to relieve the transit authority of responsibility for accident or injury
    C. refer him to the director of public relations
    D. direct him to the office of the transit authority's general counsel

31. A Sunday schedule is to be operated on a particular holiday. This schedule, in part, calls for buses to leave a certain terminal at 8:00, 8:10, 8:20, 8:28, 8:36, 8:44, 8:52, and 9:00 A.M.
    If there is a shortage of operators so that two of these runs must be dropped, the sequence of departure times that would result in the BEST service to passengers is: 8:00, _____, and 9:00.  31._____

    A. 8:12, 8:24, 8:36, 8:48      B. 8:14, 8:28, 8:40, 8:52
    C. 8:10, 8:20, 8:33, 8:47      D. 8:14, 8:28, 8:44, 8:52

32. Certain bulletin orders are reissued periodically. The BEST reason for such periodic reissuance is to  32._____

    A. notify operators of changes in the schedule of working conditions
    B. call operators' attention to changes in the motor vehicle law

C. alert operators to situations which the individual operator meets infrequently
D. inform operators of the details of a forthcoming line pick

33. Where four bus lines for different destinations start from the same subway terminal, planning is necessary to avoid passengers' embarking on the wrong bus.
The LEAST practical procedure would be to

   A. have a public address system installed in the subway mezzanine
   B. have each operator announce the destination of his bus as passengers embark
   C. station four dispatchers in the subway mezzanine to direct passengers
   D. place direction signs in the subway mezzanine

34. The time when a bus should be removed from service to be inspected and overhauled is GENERALLY determined by the number of _____ since the last inspection.

   A. round trips made
   B. trouble reports turned in
   C. months that have passed
   D. miles run

35. The safe speed on any road regardless of weather conditions is primarily a function of the ability of the vehicle operator to compensate for roadway and traffic conditions.
This statement means MOST NEARLY that it is

   A. permitted to drive a bus faster than the posted or allowable speed to compensate for traffic delays
   B. necessary for a bus operator to use his judgment to determine the safe operating speed
   C. not safe to drive at the maximum posted or allowable speed under the worst weather conditions
   D. always safe to drive well below the posted or allowable speed

36. During the rush hour, 12 buses are operated per hour in one direction, and during non-rush hours the service is reduced to 9 buses every two hours.
The average change in headway, in minutes, is MOST NEARLY

   A. 13   B. 8   C. 6   D. 2

37. A passenger comes to your depot and insists that he wants to file a claim against the transit authority.
No natter what the reason, your BEST procedure is to

   A. try to discourage the passenger in his desire to file a complaint
   B. direct the passenger to the transit authority claims department
   C. help the passenger write up the complaint and ask him to mail it in
   D. have the passenger wait in the depot while you get it touch with your superior

38. As a dispatcher, one of the BEST ways of cooperating with your superior would be to

   A. constantly acquaint him with all the details of your job
   B. submit all problems about the work to him for his decision
   C. accept full responsibility for the work assigned to you
   D. never submit a problem about the work to him for his decision

39. In deciding what to do about a newly appointed operator who was guilty of a minor violation, it would be BEST for a dispatcher assigned as location chief to FIRST

    A. consult with several other operators who know him well
    B. speak to the operator involved in private
    C. tell the man in the presence of other operators that you intend to make an example of him
    D. issue a memo to all operators in the depot explaining the prescribed penalty for this violation

39.____

40. In making studies to determine adequacy of service on a bus line, it is MOST important for a checker stationed at a point on the line to record the number of

    A. passengers alighting from each bus
    B. buses more than one interval behind schedule
    C. buses more than one interval ahead of schedule
    D. passengers carried on each bus

40.____

41. Only nine buses are available for a route on which the terminal-to-terminal running time is fifty-one minutes. The MINIMUM operable headway is CLOSEST to _____ minutes.

    A. 5      B. 6      C. 10      D. 12

41.____

42. When an operator is involved in an accident, it is the duty of the location chief to

    A. go to the scene of the accident and direct the investigation
    B. discuss the accident with the operator and point out corrective action
    C. make out the accident report required by state law
    D. send the operator to the accident prevention supervisor for reinstruction

42.____

43. On his run-off to the depot after dark, the operator in every case is required to

    A. run empty with bus *dark* so that he can see the road clearly
    B. carry passengers from point where run-off leaves bus route to depot
    C. carry passengers from terminal to point where runoff leaves bus route
    D. run empty with bus illuminated

43.____

44. It is MOST likely that bus service would be curtailed during a

    A. fog                B. snow storm
    C. cold spell         D. thunderstorm

44.____

45. The extra amount paid an operator for any day on which he has newly appointed student operators under instruction

    A. depends on the length of time that instructions are given
    B. varies with the number of students
    C. is a fixed amount
    D. depends on the number of trips to which student operators are assigned

45.____

46. Assume that after your promotion, you find that one of the men who reports to you resents your authority because he had longer service than you but was not reached for appointment.
    In this case, you should

46.____

A. do nothing about it for a time giving his resentment a chance to wear off
B. ask to have this man transferred to another depot
C. let him do your work at every opportunity
D. frequently ask his advice in emergencies

47. Because the bus on which you are riding has made two hard stops, causing some standing passengers to fall and putting considerable strain on the other standing passengers to retain their balance, you identify yourself to the operator and question him. He claims that the brakes grab.
As a dispatcher, you should

   A. drive the bus yourself for a few stops to see how the brakes set
   B. tell the operator to call the control desk, transfer his passengers, and take the bus out of service
   C. tell the operator to proceed much slower and report the bad brakes at the terminal
   D. tell the operator to proceed slowly while you get off and report the condition to the control desk

48. If the fare box register on a bus shows $53.00 upon return to the depot, it can reasonably be concluded that MOST likely

   A. some of the passengers were school children
   B. the fare box was not registering properly
   C. one or more passengers did not deposit the correct fare
   D. among the passengers carried was a small group traveling on permit

49. Your BEST course of action if your relief frequently reports ten to fifteen minutes late is to

   A. come late yourself sometimes to make up the time
   B. put in a claim for overtime for the extra time
   C. say nothing to your relief but report the matter to the general superintendent
   D. give your relief fair warning that you will report him if his lateness continues

50. An operator who keeps his engine running for more than three minutes while standing at a terminal is NOT subject on that account to

   A. disciplinary action by the transit authority
   B. citation by the department of air pollution control
   C. fines imposed by the court of jurisdiction
   D. arrest by a police officer

# KEY (CORRECT ANSWERS)

| | | | | |
|---|---|---|---|---|
| 1. C | 11. D | 21. D | 31. A | 41. D |
| 2. D | 12. C | 22. A | 32. C | 42. B |
| 3. C | 13. B | 23. C | 33. C | 43. D |
| 4. A | 14. C | 24. D | 34. D | 44. B |
| 5. B | 15. A | 25. C | 35. B | 45. C |
| 6. C | 16. D | 26. D | 36. B | 46. A |
| 7. A | 17. B | 27. A | 37. B | 47. B |
| 8. A | 18. B | 28. A | 38. C | 48. C |
| 9. D | 19. C | 29. D | 39. B | 49. D |
| 10. B | 20. C | 30. C | 40. D | 50. D |

# TEST 2

DIRECTIONS: Each question or incomplete statement is followed by several suggested answers or completions. Select the one that BEST answers the question or completes the statement. *PRINT THE LETTER OF THE CORRECT ANSWER IN THE SPACE AT THE RIGHT.*

1. The function of a dispatcher which can NOT be delegated to an operator is

    A. re-routing buses at the scene of a fire
    B. handling discipline
    C. inspection of uniforms
    D. noting arrival times of buses at a time point

1.____

2. The MOST probable result of operating a bus ahead of schedule would be

    A. inconvenience to the passengers on the bus
    B. overloading the following bus
    C. requests that the faster schedule be standardized
    D. that the bus ahead of schedule would pick up more than a normal load

2.____

3. After your appointment as a dispatcher, you find that too much of your time is spent in maintaining the records which were kept by the dispatcher who had the job before you. In this case, you should

    A. get together with your superior and decide whether all these records are necessary
    B. turn the record keeping over to a light duty line operator
    C. discontinue for a while those records which you believe are unnecessary and see how it works
    D. work on the extra records after working hours

3.____

4. While on duty, road dispatchers must wear the prescribed uniform.
   In this connection, it is permitted to wear

    A. a sweater under the uniform coat
    B. sleeve garters on the outside of uniform jacket sleeves
    C. a uniform hat with ventilating holes cut in it
    D. uniform trousers with cuffs

4.____

5. The stop signal becomes inoperative shortly after a bus leaves the terminal.
   The operator should

    A. transfer his passengers to the next bus and return to the depot
    B. telephone the depot dispatcher and ask for instructions
    C. try to locate and fix the trouble
    D. ask the passengers to call out their stops

5.____

6. If a dispatcher riding the line notices an operator closing the door of his bus too soon as passengers alight, the MOST appropriate action for the dispatcher to take would be to

    A. take over the operation of the bus himself to illustrate proper door closing
    B. explain to the operator how the door should be closed before allowing him to continue

6.____

C. take no immediate action but speak to the operator at the end of his tour and explain his mistakes
D. reprimand the operator and report him to the senior dispatcher for action

7. As an aid in ascertaining the identity of students guilty of rowdyism and vandalism, a reissued bulletin order requires that operators note the names of

   A. the first two students who board bus with student cards
   B. all the students who board the bus with student cards
   C. the schools attended by most of the students who board the bus
   D. at least two adult passengers to act as witnesses in case of trouble

8. *Shimmy* in a bus is PROBABLY due to

   A. front tires being worn smooth
   B. front spring failure on one side
   C. carrying too many passengers
   D. an imbalanced front wheel

9. With respect to tokens deposited in the fare box, operators are instructed to

   A. keep them and turn them in with the day's receipts
   B. use them in making change
   C. offer them for cash to passengers going to the subway
   D. return them to the passengers depositing them and request cash

10. The classification of an accident in which a truck was struck by a bus would be *Collision* followed by the letters

    A. B & B    B. B & V    C. V & B    D. TAV & V

11. One POSITIVE advantage of the rear mounted bus engine is that

    A. interior heating of the bus is simplified
    B. overheating of the engine is avoided
    C. it makes rear-wheel drive possible
    D. it makes better use of available chassis space

12. The motor vehicle bureau's point system is SPECIFICALLY designed to penalize the driver who

    A. is too young or too old
    B. does not maintain his car properly
    C. repeatedly violates traffic laws
    D. does not keep up to date on traffic regulations

13. A few days after a system-wide order which affects mainly bus operators is issued, several operators complain to you that the order is not clear or fair.
    The POOREST action for you to take in this case would be to

    A. ignore the operators' complaints
    B. insist that the order be followed until further notice
    C. ask other operators for their opinions
    D. bring the controversial order to the attention of your superiors

14. Certain bulletin orders are reissued periodically. One that is NOT so reissued is the one that

    A. cautions operators on safe procedures in reverse movements of buses
    B. calls the attention of operators to a new traffic regulation
    C. directs operators to comply with air pollution control regulations
    D. informs operators of the rules relating to one bus passing another

15. In cases involving minor infractions of the rules and regulations by newly appointed operators, the dispatcher should

    A. treat the new operators no differently from experienced ones
    B. overlook all such infractions for a short time
    C. enter every infraction on the operator's record
    D. point out the particular infraction but take no other action

16. When an unusual emergency arises and it would take too long to contact a superior to check the method of handling the situation, the BEST procedure is to

    A. act according to experience and your own best judgment
    B. telephone and confer with another dispatcher
    C. confer with your operators
    D. take no action

17. A passenger complains to you at a field check point that a particular newly appointed operator is rude in his attitude.
    Your BEST action as a dispatcher would be to tell the passenger you will take care of the matter and

    A. explain to the passenger that the man is new
    B. ask him to put his complaint in writing
    C. report the operator to the dispatcher in charge
    D. speak to the operator later to get his story

18. A bus leaves one time point at 10:35 and arrives at the next time point at 11:00. If the distance between the time points is 3 miles, the average speed of the bus, in MPH, was MOST NEARLY

    A. 6    B. 6 1/2    C. 7    D. 7 1/2

19. Certain lost articles are required to be forwarded to the lost property office by special messenger as soon as possible instead of being held for the regular lost property pick up.
    One such article would be a

    A. loaded revolver
    B. lady's pocketbook containing jewelry
    C. box camera
    D. bag containing sliced meat and cheese

20. Assume you are located at a depot and notice that a certain operator is holding a handkerchief over one eye as he signs in. When you question him, he says that *something blew into* his eye while on his way to work but that *it seems to be getting better*.
    In this case, it would show GOOD judgment if you had the operator

A. sit down while you tried to remove the particle from his eye
B. take out his bus if he felt able
C. sign out sick and sent him home
D. wait in the depot and you checked the condition again a short time later

21. The power to revoke a license to drive a motor vehicle is in the hands of the

   A. transit authority
   B. police commissioner
   C. traffic commissioner
   D. commissioner of motor vehicles

22. The MAXIMUM number of children under six years of age which may be carried free on the lines of the transit authority when accompanied by one adult is

   A. 1  B. 2  C. 3  D. 4

23. The result of running with low engine oil pressure is MOST likely to be

   A. damage to the equipment        B. slow braking
   C. faulty steering                D. low fuel mileage

24. Assume that there are 300 bus operators at terminal A. Terninal B has 85% as many bus operators as terminal A, and terminal C has 90% as many bus operators as terminal B. The number of operators assigned to terminal C is NEAREST to

   A. 230  B. 245  C. 255  D. 270

25. An ADVANTAGE of diesel engine buses over gasoline engine buses is that the

   A. engine exhaust is less poisonous
   B. cost for fuel is lower
   C. diesel bus can go faster
   D. diesel engine is easier to operate

26. A bus leaves the terminal on time at 11:48 A.M. and after one round trip returns 11 minutes late at 1:06 P.M. It leaves again on time at 1:12 P.M.
If the scheduled recovery time at both ends of the line is the same, the scheduled terminal-to-terminal running time, in minutes, is

   A. 25  B. 33  C. 42  D. 50

27. It would be LEAST important for a dispatcher stationed at a time point to observe the

   A. destination signs on buses
   B. approximate number of passengers getting on or off buses
   C. position of buses making the stop
   D. size of the buses

28. The present schedule of a particular bus line provides for buses on a 5-minute headway. If this schedule is changed to a 4-minute headway, the number of buses per hour will be

   A. decreased by 3        B. decreased by 4
   C. increased by 3        D. increased by 4

29. A bus line had a schedule headway of 6 minutes. Run #7 left the near terminal at 10:45 A.M. and shortly thereafter had to be taken out of service on account of engine trouble. Its passengers were picked up by its follower, run #8. The delay caused run #8 to arrive at the far terminal 6 minutes late.
If the time of arrival of run #8 was 11:53 A.M., then the scheduled running time for the trip was _____ minutes.

    A. 44  B. 56  C. 68  D. 96

30. The violation committed by an operator that places the transit authority in the LEAST defensible position in the event of an accident is

    A. falling behind the schedule
    B. stopping to accept or discharge passengers at other than regular designated stops
    C. refusing to accept regular transit system subway tokens
    D. failing to call out a stop for a requested location

31. The type of pick that is required to be held if 5 additional runs are added to one line out of a depot serving 25 lines is a _____ pick.

    A. system  B. depot  C. line  D. division

32. A defective piece of equipment which would require that the bus be taken out of service immediately is a(n)

    A. illegible side destination marker
    B. blown lamp bulb in an interior lighting circuit
    C. improperly operating stop light
    D. broken seat

33. It is the responsibility of dispatchers assigned to duty where there is no property protection to inspect periodically the buses stored outside of garage buildings.
Such periodic tours of inspection should take place AT LEAST every _____ hour(s).

    A. 1  B. 2  C. 3  D. 4

34. According to regulations, the MAXIMUM time that a bus engine may run idle while standing at the end of a line is _____ minute(s).

    A. 1  B. 2  C. 3  D. 4

35. Power from the storage battery on a bus is NOT used to operate the

    A. lights
    B. doors
    C. starter
    D. heater fan

36. A dispatcher would be using GOOD judgment if, during a very heavy fog, he

    A. sent out more than the regular number of buses
    B. sent out fewer than the regular number of buses
    C. kept all the buses in the depot
    D. instructed the operators to drive at slow speed

37. It would be necessary for a dispatcher to obtain approval from his superior before 37.____

    A. arranging with his relief to leave an hour earlier the next day
    B. calling the transit police in an emergency
    C. giving one of his operators a deserved reprimand
    D. denying an unfit operator permission to take a bus out of the depot

38. A dispatcher notices an unusually large number of passengers boarding the buses at a 38.____
    particular stop on one of the lines for several successive days.
    In this case, he would do BEST, as a FIRST step, to

    A. make a note of this situation and see how long it continues
    B. check on the area near the stop to see if there have been any building or use changes
    C. assign light duty men to make an exact count of the passengers boarding and alighting
    D. call the office and inquire as to the cause of this change in riding

39. One GOOD way to have transit employees as a whole learn good safety habits is to 39.____

    A. let them learn through their own mistakes
    B. offer prizes for the best safety records
    C. make them study the rules during their spare time
    D. penalize them with loss of pay for lost-time accidents

40. If it is extremely important to be certain that all operators have seen a temporary special 40.____
    order, the BEST procedure is to

    A. read the order to each operator as he signs in
    B. have the order state that each operator should confirm by calling the office of the superintendent
    C. issue a copy to each operator with instructions to keep it on his person
    D. post it on the depot bulletin board and have each reporting operator sign the log

41. During the month of August, approximately 900,000 more passengers used the surface 41.____
    lines than during the same month the year before. This was an increase of about 3%.
    The total number of passengers who used this surface transportation system during
    August was NEAREST to

    A. 3,000,000                B. 3,900,000
    C. 29,000,000               D. 31,000,000

42. If an operator with a poor accident record picked onto your line, you would be using 42.____
    GOOD judgment if you

    A. suggested he pick a vacation relief trick
    B. warned the operator that you would tolerate no accidents in which he was involved
    C. checked with the safety and accident prevention supervisor
    D. told him that you were aware of his accident record and were keeping an eye on him

43. The case that is likely to result in the LEAST severe penalty against an operator is 43.____

    A. reporting for duty under the influence of alcohol
    B. absenting himself from duty without prior notification

C. depositing the fares in the fare box himself when giving change
D. sustaining rear end bus damage to his bus after collision with a passenger car

44. The absentee report kept at the depot does NOT include absences charged to

   A. sick leave
   B. R.D.O
   C. A.V.A.
   D. jury duty

45. About noon on a rainy weekday, an operator on a line where a trip is about one hour reports by telephone that his front door has become inoperative about halfway to the terminal furthest from the depot.
It would probably be BEST to instruct him to transfer his passengers to the next bus and

   A. wait where he is for a repairman
   B. continue to the far terminal where a repairman will meet him
   C. return the bus to the depot for repairs
   D. return to the depot for reassignment, leaving the bus closed where it is

46. If the operator referred to in the preceding question reported that his rear door had become inoperative but that his front door was operating satisfactorily, it would probably be BEST to instruct him to

   A. continue in service making normal stops to the far terminal
   B. continue to the far terminal stopping only to discharge passengers
   C. transfer his passengers to the next bus and wait for a repairman
   D. transfer his passengers to the next bus and return his bus to the depot

47. If a passenger claims a package which has been turned in to you in the field, it is NOT necessary for you to have the passenger

   A. identify himself
   B. sign a receipt
   C. describe the contents before opening the package
   D. sign a waiver of claim against the transit authority

48. When an operator has determined that it is safe to back up a bus, he will signal by tooting his horn before starting the reverse movement.
The CORRECT number of toots to blow is

   A. 1    B. 2    C. 3    D. 4

49. The employee who opens a first aid kit must make an immediate report on a prescribed form.
Such report would NOT show the

   A. name of the employee opening the kit
   B. last previous date on which the kit was used
   C. purpose for which the materials therein were used
   D. amount of first aid material used

50. As a dispatcher at a location where the wheels of a bus are stuck in deep snow, you would be giving the operator of the bus GOOD advice if you told him to

    A. accelerate slowly
    B. accelerate rapidly
    C. have the passengers move to the rear
    D. have the passengers move to the front

50.____

---

## KEY (CORRECT ANSWERS)

| | | | | | | | | | |
|---|---|---|---|---|---|---|---|---|---|
| 1. | B | 11. | D | 21. | D | 31. | C | 41. | D |
| 2. | B | 12. | C | 22. | C | 32. | C | 42. | C |
| 3. | A | 13. | A | 23. | A | 33. | B | 43. | D |
| 4. | A | 14. | B | 24. | A | 34. | C | 44. | B |
| 5. | D | 15. | D | 25. | B | 35. | B | 45. | C |
| 6. | B | 16. | A | 26. | A | 36. | D | 46. | A |
| 7. | A | 17. | D | 27. | D | 37. | A | 47. | D |
| 8. | D | 18. | C | 28. | C | 38. | B | 48. | C |
| 9. | A | 19. | B | 29. | B | 39. | B | 49. | B |
| 10. | B | 20. | D | 30. | B | 40. | D | 50. | A |

# TEST 3

DIRECTIONS: Each question or incomplete statement is followed by several suggested answers or completions. Select the one that BEST answers the question or completes the statement. *PRINT THE LETTER OF THE CORRECT ANSWER IN THE SPACE AT THE RIGHT.*

1. Assume that, as a dispatcher, you have received an assignment from your superior to supervise the operation of several special buses due to a one-d.ay event. In your opinion, the buses assigned are too small for this operation.
   In this case, you SHOULD

   A. refuse to take the assignment as given
   B. carry out the job to the best of your ability with the buses assigned
   C. substitute larger buses for those assigned without bothering your superior
   D. call your doubts to the attention of the superior as soon as possible

2. For making field checks of adequacy of service on a particular bus route, it is MOST essential for the dispatcher to know in advance the

   A. scheduled headway          B. bus capacity
   C. route mileage              D. scheduled running time

3. Suppose that one of your operators is accidentally injured on the job.
   In your report on the accident, it is LEAST important to include the

   A. operator's general attitude toward the department
   B. kind of injury and parts of the body involved
   C. kind of work the operator was doing when the accident occurred
   D. time and place of the accident

4. In computing bus mileage, it is NOT necessary to include the distance of

   A. run-ons or run-offs
   B. deviations from scheduled routes
   C. movements between garages
   D. movements within a shop

5. The trip report portions of the combined register card and trip report are separated from the register cards and sorted into two groups for forwarding.
   One of these two groups is those cards which show

   A. skipped stops              B. deviations from schedule
   C. no-passenger trips         D. traffic delays

6. One standard operating procedure reads, *No regular operator shall be assigned to full run either as a double-up or on his regular day off in preference to extra operator standing for work.*
   According to this procedure, when an extra operator is available, a regular operator must NOT be

   A. given an extra trip on completing his run
   B. assigned a full run
   C. given work on his day off
   D. assigned a special

7. A run is NOT considered open when the operator assigned to the run has

   A. transferred to another depot
   B. been promoted to a higher title
   C. resigned from the service
   D. been absent on sick leave for 30 consecutive days

8. It would be LEAST important for a dispatcher, in the routine performance of his duties, to

   A. concentrate on keeping buses on schedule
   B. know when a situation requires a decision from higher authority
   C. be thoroughly familiar with the bus routes in his area
   D. be thoroughly familiar with the operators on his line

9. On inspecting his bus at the end of a trip, an operator finds a student's wallet containing, among other things, a reduced fare privilege card.
   The operator should

   A. return the wallet and card to the student identified on the card
   B. turn the wallet and card in at the depot as a single item
   C. turn the wallet and card in at the depot as two items
   D. take the wallet and card directly to the lost property office

10. If an operator observes a taxicab competing with transit authority buses, he is required to furnish a report to the location chief giving all information.
    A bit of information NOT specifically required on this report is the

    A. date and time of observation
    B. name of the cab company
    C. name of the taxidriver
    D. number of passengers in the cab

11. When the heat indicator gage on the dash of a bus registers 212°, or when the telltale light and buzzer indicate that the engine is overheated, the

    A. bus must be operated slowly for a while
    B. engine must be raced until it cools
    C. engine must be allowed to idle until it cools
    D. bus must not be continued in operation

12. On some buses, the generator main fuses have been replaced by a circuit breaker.
    The MOST likely reason for this changeover is that

    A. better battery protection is obtained
    B. it eliminates fire hazard
    C. resetting the breaker is easier than replacing a fuse
    D. higher generator output is secured

13. An operator notices that he must make increasingly heavier brake applications when braking his bus at regular stops.
    The BEST action is for the operator to

    A. drive slowly
    B. use the hand brake in conjunction with the pedal

C. report this condition at his first opportunity
D. discharge his passengers and return to the depot

14. Regular letter carriers within certain areas are carried on the surface lines without payment of fare, provided they have three items of identification.
These three items are

   A. bag, badge, and uniform
   B. uniform, cap, and badge
   C. bag, uniform, and cap
   D. cap, badge, and bag

14.____

15. The senior transportation department supervisory member at the scene of an emergency is required to assume direction of all activities in coping with the emergency. Seniority for this purpose is determined by

   A. title
   B. years in the department
   C. designation by the assistant general superintendent
   D. agreement

15.____

16. Five minutes before its scheduled arrival at a midtown terminal during the morning rush hours, a certain bus is 12 stops away.
It is MOST likely to be true that this bus

   A. was dispatched late
   B. will arrive late
   C. was dispatched early
   D. will arrive early

16.____

17. The trait in a dispatcher that is MOST likely to win the respect of the operators he supervises is

   A. applying the letter of the rules in all cases
   B. overlooking minor violations
   C. handling the various situations promptly as they arise
   D. being pleasant to all operators at all times

17.____

18. Every accident must be discussed with the operator involved by the

   A. terminal dispatcher
   B. location chief
   C. safety coordinator
   D. labor relations assistant

18.____

19. An operator shows his depot supervisor a system pick slip which schedules the operator to pick during his working time.
The supervisor should arrange for a

   A. day off charged against A.V.A. days
   B. change in regular assignment or R.D.O.
   C. change in picking time
   D. leave of absence with pay

19.____

20. When an operator reports late due to his own delinquency, the dispatcher may NOT

   A. assign him to the balance of his own run
   B. give him another complete run
   C. hold him longer than one hour without pay
   D. release him before the expiration of one hour

20.____

21. Part of the time of supervision is spent in investigating complaints by passengers against operators.
    The BEST basic solution to the problem is to

    A. send a standard courteous answer to each complaint but omit investigation unless the complaint is repeated
    B. educate passengers to the fact that investigating complaints is expensive
    C. have supervision stress courtesy in public relations
    D. investigate only the legitimate complaints

21.____

22. One reason for splitting the bus headway is that

    A. a run has been omitted
    B. the regular schedule has been prepared incorrectly
    C. short runs may be maintained
    D. too much overtime is being earned

22.____

23. The action of a bus operator which causes the GREATEST discomfort to passengers is

    A. slowness in making change
    B. making fast starts and stops
    C. stopping away from the curb
    D. falling behind schedule

23.____

24. The BEST test of a dispatcher's supervisory skills is

    A. the absorption of several new operators under his supervision because some headways were reduced
    B. trying to get operators to use the increased schedule running time during certain hours
    C. taking over the assignment of a dispatcher who has retired
    D. maintaining operators' interest in public relations

24.____

25. The investigation of an accident would be considered successful if

    A. it was found that the transit authority was not responsible for the accident
    B. it was determined that damage to any bus was minor
    C. no transit employee lost working time
    D. information was obtained which will help prevent future accidents

25.____

26. An operator, making his last trip for the day, notices that the reading of the engine oil pressure gage has dropped to zero when he is about one mile from the depot which is the end of his run.
    After the operator explains this to you over the telephone, you would do BEST to tell him to

    A. *proceed* to the depot at normal speed since he is only one mile away
    B. *proceed* to the depot at slow speed to reduce possibility of bus damage
    C. *stay* with his bus until you send a repair crew and a bus to pick up his passengers
    D. *stay* at the telephone for further instructions while you arrange for relief

26.____

27. When insufficient operators are available on a paid holiday to cover all runs, the dispatcher may  27.____

    A. assign licensed maintainers to the open runs
    B. order certain operators on duty under threat of suspension
    C. cover the open runs with supervisors
    D. drop certain runs and patch schedules

28. As supervisor of a newly appointed bus operator, you should expect him to  28.____

    A. pay close attention to your instructions
    B. complete his runs ahead of time to make an impression
    C. make plenty of mistakes
    D. quickly learn his rights as an employee

29. According to standard operating procedures, upon completion of six days of preliminary instructions at the schoolroom, each student operator is required to report to his assigned depot and perform all his duties as an operator under the direction of the instructing operator who is required to report daily on each student's progress. The road training time depends MAINLY on each student's ability and the  29.____

    A. number of students
    B. ability of the instructor
    C. number of routes
    D. availability of buses

Questions 30-50.

DIRECTIONS: Questions 30 through 50, inclusive, are based on the schedule shown on the following page. Consult this schedule in answering these questions.

## WEEKLY SCHEDULE

| Run | Report | | | | | | | | | | | | | | | | Clear | Trips | Speed | Sw. ing | Travel | Vehicle | All-ow-ance | Paid Sw. ing | Pct. |
|---|---|---|---|---|---|---|---|---|---|---|---|---|---|---|---|---|---|---|---|---|---|---|---|---|
| | **AM** | | | | | | | | | | | | | | | | | | | | | | | |
| 1 | 430 | Out 440 | 448 518 | 554 624 | 709 734 | 808 843 | | Off 920 | (R/9)1027 | 1033 1108 | 1144 347 | | | 1205 | 10 | | | | 811 |
| 2 | 445 | Out 455 | 503 533 | 604 636 | 713 748 | 823 858 | | Off 935 | (R/13)1018 | 1019 1054 | 1129 1204 | 1233 (R/8) | | 1256 | 12 | 811 | 35 | 16 | 655 | 25 | 59 | 811 |
| 3 | 500 | Out 510 | 518 548 | 624 656 | 728 803 | 838 913 | 948 (R/5) | | (R/14)1038 | 1040 1115 | 1150 1225 | 1257 (R/10) | | | | | | | | | | | |
| 11 | 715 | Out 725 | 733 808 | 843 918 | RO 947 (R/2) | RO 955 | | (R/4)1102 | 1108 1143 | 1218 1253 | 128 203 | 237 (R/18) | | 300 | 10 | 745 | 59 | 16 | 605 | 40 | 59 | 803 |
| 12 | 725 | Out 735 | 743 818 | 855 930 | 1005 1040 | 1115 1150 | 1221 (R/14) | | (R/6) 200 | 203 238 | 313 348 | 423 458 | 527 (R/18) | 550 | 14 | 1025 | | | 813 | | 49 | |
| 13 | 740 | Out 750 | 758 833 | 909 944 | 1018 (R/2) | | | (R/10)1203 | 1204 1239 | 114 149 | 224 259 | 334 409 | 438 (R/16) | 501 | 12 | | | | | | | |
| | **PM** | | | | | | | | | | | | | | | | | | | | | | | |
| 17 | 158 | (R/7)216 | 217 252 | 327 402 | 437 512 | 623 | RO 652 | | (R/22)757 | 759 834 | 912 947 | 1016 (R/27) | | 1039 | 12 | | | | | | | 812 |
| 18 | 219 | (R/11)237 | 238 313 | 348 423 | 455 (R/23) | | | (R/12)527 | 533 608 | 642 717 | 752 827 | 904 939 | 1013 (R/30) | 1036 | 12 | 817 | 32 | 16 | 704 | 25 | 32 | 812 |
| 20 | 238 | (R/8)256 | 259 334 | 409 444 | 518 553 | 628 703 | RO 732 | | (R/24)831 | 834 909 | 944 1019 | 1049 (R/25) | | 1112 | 12 | 834 | 43 | 24 | 702 | 25 | 43 | 834 |
| 21 | 245 | (R/15)303 | 306 341 | 416 451 | 528 603 | 632 | Off 640 | (R/19)735 | 738 813 | 848 923 | 1000 1035 | RO 1104 | Off 1112 | 1127 | 12 | 842 | 47 | 16 | 714 | 25 | 47 | 842 |
| 29 | 907 | (R/16)925 | 928 1003 | 1040 115 | 1144 | Off 1152 | (R/30)1236 | 1236 113 | 148 221 | 258 328 | 358 428 | RO 454 | Off 502 | 517 | 12 | 810 | 36 | | 655 | 25 | 35 | 810 |
| 30 | 955 | (R/18)1013 | 1016 1051 | 1128 1203 | 1236 (R/29) | | (R/25)118 | 124 157 | 228 258 | 328 358 | 428 458 | 524 | Off 532 | 547 | 12 | 752 | 42 | 8 | | 25 | | 800 |

Notes: 
(1) The travel allowance for reliefs made away from the depot is 8 minutes.
(2) The number of route-miles for this bus line is 5.1 miles.
(3) The number of route-miles in run-on or run-off trips is 1.1 miles.
(4) The scheduled terminal-to-terminal time is 26 minutes from 1:00 A.M. to 6:00 A.M., and 29 minutes at other times.

7 (#3)

30. The operator who has MOST run-on and run-off trips is the one on Run No.   30.____
    A. 11           B. 12           C. 13           D. 17

31. The Spread for Run No. 1, in hours and minutes, is   31.____
    A. 5:55         B. 6:34         C. 7:35         D. 8:00

32. The Paid Swing for Run No. 13 is _____ minutes.   32.____
    A. 0            B. 45           C. 49           D. 60

33. The Pay for Run No. 13, in hours and minutes, is   33.____
    A. 7:03         B. 8:00         C. 8:48         D. 9:21

34. The Allowance for Run No. 30 is _____ minutes.   34.____
    A. 8            B. 25           C. 33           D. 42

35. The time, in hours and minutes, that should be shown in the Pay column for Run No. 12 is   35.____
    A. 8:21         B. 8:46         C. 8:57         D. 9:09

36. The operator on Run No. 18 is relieved for his swing by the operator on Run No.   36.____
    A. 11           B. 12           C. 23           D. 30

37. One operator who starts his tour by driving his bus from the depot to the terminal, and who is relieved for his swing at the terminal, is the operator on Run No.   37.____
    A. 1            B. 2            C. 3            D. 11

38. The TOTAL travel time allowed for Run No. 17 is _____ minutes.   38.____
    A. 0            B. 8            C. 16           D. 24

39. The travel time allowed for Run No. 12 between the beginning and the end of the swing is _____ minutes.   39.____
    A. 0            B. 3            C. 8            D. 16

40. The travel time allowed for Run No. 18 at the end of the tour is _____ minutes.   40.____
    A. 0            B. 8            C. 23           D. 25

41. The recovery time for the operator of Run No. 20 at the end of his first trip is _____ minutes.   41.____
    A. 3            B. 6            C. 9            D. 12

42. The recovery time for the operator of Run No. 30 at the end of his first trip after swinging is _____ minutes.   42.____
    A. 4            B. 5            C. 6            D. 7

43. The schedule speed for this line at noon is CLOSEST to _____ MPH.   43.____
    A. 5.3          B. 5.7          C. 10.6         D. 11.8

44. The eight minutes travel time allowed for Run No. 30 is for travel from 44._____

    A. depot to relief point at beginning of tour
    B. depot to relief point after swing
    C. relief point to depot before swing
    D. relief point to depot at end of tour

45. The time added to the normal reporting clearing allowance to bring the Pay for Run No. 45._____
    11 up to 8 hours is _____ minutes.

    A. 15         B. 16         C. 25         D. 40

46. The ACTUAL amount of overtime for which Run No. 17 pays time-and-a-half is _____ 46._____
    minutes.

    A. 0          B. 14         C. 27         D. 41

47. On Run No. 2, the operator actually drives the buses each day for a total distance, in 47._____
    miles, of

    A. 61.2       B. 62.3       C. 63.4       D. 64.5

48. The Pay for Run No. 21 does not include overtime at time-and-a-half because, in com- 48._____
    puting overtime,

    A. allowance cannot exceed 25 minutes
    B. vehicle time must be 8 hours
    C. paid swing is not included
    D. travel time must be included

49. The headway operated on this line between 2:30 and 4:30 A.M. is about _____ min- 49._____
    utes.

    A. 60         B. 45         C. 30         D. 15

50. At $11.32 per hour, working a 5-day week, the regular weekly earnings for Run No. 20 are 50._____

    A. $472.04    B. $484.88    C. $497.72    D. $510.56

# KEY (CORRECT ANSWERS)

| | | | | |
|---|---|---|---|---|
| 1. D | 11. D | 21. C | 31. C | 41. B |
| 2. B | 12. C | 22. C | 32. A | 42. D |
| 3. A | 13. C | 23. B | 33. B | 43. C |
| 4. D | 14. D | 24. D | 34. C | 44. A |
| 5. B | 15. A | 25. D | 35. D | 45. A |
| 6. B | 16. B | 26. C | 36. C | 46. A |
| 7. D | 17. C | 27. D | 37. C | 47. C |
| 8. D | 18. B | 28. A | 38. D | 48. C |
| 9. B | 19. B | 29. C | 39. A | 49. C |
| 10. C | 20. C | 30. A | 40. B | 50. B |

# EXAMINATION SECTION
# TEST 1

DIRECTIONS: Each question or incomplete statement is followed by several suggested answers or completions. Select the one that BEST answers the question or completes the statement. *PRINT THE LETTER OF THE CORRECT ANSWER IN THE SPACE AT THE RIGHT.*

Questions 1-10.

DIRECTIONS: Questions 1 through 10 are based on the sample schedule below. Refer to this schedule when answering these questions. Assume that all operations proceed as scheduled unless otherwise stated in the question.

JACK DEPOT

ROUTE: T-5 DOG AVE.
WEEKDAY SCHEDULE NO. Y-4
EFFECTIVE: 4/26

RUNNING TIME
From Pick St. and from Bart St.

|  | 6:00 AM 3:00 PM | 3:00 PM 6:00 AM |
|---|---|---|
| Pick St. | - | - |
| Lane St. | 7 min. | 6 min. |
| May St. | 13 min. | 10 min. |
| John St. | 14 min. | 11 min. |
| Card St. | 6 min. | 5 min. |
| Pal St. | 8 min. | 6 min. |
| Mud St. | 12 min. | 10 min. |
| Bart St. | 9 min. | 8 min. |
| Totals | 69 min. | 56 min. |

HEADWAYS
From Pick St. and from Bart St.

| 12:00 Mid. | - |
| 6:00 A.M. | 30 min. |
| 9:00 A.M. | 15 min. |
| 3:00 P.M. | 20 min. |
| 6:00 P.M. | 15 min. |
| 12:00 Mid. | 25 min. |

NORTHBOUND BUSES LEAVE FROM PICK ST.
SOUTHBOUND BUSES LEAVE FROM BART ST.

NOTE: IN ACCORDANCE WITH THIS SCHEDULE, A NORTHBOUND BUS IS SCHEULED TO LEAVE FROM PICK ST. AT 1:00 P.M.

1. The buses leaving Pick Street at 1:40 P.M. and at 2:20 P.M. should arrive at Mud Street _____ minutes apart.   1._____

   A. 20     B. 35     C. 36     D. 40

2. The TOTAL number of northbound buses that should be traveling enroute between Pick Street and Bart Street any time between 3:00 P.M. and 3:30 P.M. is   2._____

   A. 2     B. 3     C. 4     D. 5

3. The bus leaving Pick Street at 2:40 P.M. should arrive at Bart Street at _____ P.M.

   A. 3:42   B. 3:40   C. 3:38   D. 3:36

4. If the northbound bus leaving Pick Street at 2:20 P.M. is delayed at May Street for 20 minutes, it should arrive at Pal Street at _____ P.M.

   A. 3:22   B. 3:23   C. 3:25   D. 3:26

5. If the layover time at Bart Street is 6 minutes, a bus leaving Pick Street at 2:00 P.M. should leave Bart Street for its return trip to Pick Street at _____ P.M.

   A. 3:08   B. 3:14   C. 3:15   D. 4:10

6. If the distance from Pick Street to Bart Street is 9.1 miles, then the bus which leaves Pick Street at 2:20 P.M. should travel the entire distance at an average speed that is CLOSEST to _____ MPH.

   A. 6 1/2   B. 8 1/2   C. 10 1/2   D. 12/1/2

7. The bus leaving May Street at 2:40 P.M. should arrive at Mud Street at _____ P.M.

   A. 3:16   B. 3:20   C. 3:32   D. 3:41

8. Between 3:00 P.M. and 4:00 P.M., there should be a northbound bus arriving at Bart Street at _____ P.M.

   A. 3:09   B. 3:29   C. 3:24   D. 3:49

9. A northbound bus arriving at Card Street at 3:20 P.M. would MOST likely be

   A. on time
   C. 3 minutes late
   B. 4 minutes late
   D. 2 minutes late

10. If the northbound bus leaving Pick Street at 2:00 P.M. is delayed for 20 minutes at John Street and takes 5 minutes less time than scheduled to run from Pal Street to Bart Street, it will arrive at Bart Street at APPROXIMATELY _____ P.M.

    A. 3:29   B. 3:24   C. 3:23   D. 3:19

11. When a bus route street is blocked by a fire engine, a dispatcher who is present at the scene should make sure that buses stop AT LEAST _____ feet from the fire engine.

    A. 50   B. 75   C. 100   D. 150

12. A man who is waiting on a long line for a bus sees you and angrily complains to you about poor bus service. Of the following, the BEST procedure for you to follow in this case is to listen to the man and

    A. tell him to complain to the head of the transit authority
    B. tell him that you are in agreement with him
    C. avoid making any argumentative statements
    D. tell him that the transit authority cannot improve bus service because of the financial crisis in the city

13. According to the book of rules and regulations, a bus operator who calls in sick must do so AT LEAST _____ hour(s) before his scheduled reporting time.   13._____

    A. 1/2   B. 1   C. 2   D. 3

14. If a bus operator is notified that he must appear in a Criminal Court on a matter pertaining to the transit system, he should IMMEDIATELY upon receipt of such notice inform   14._____

    A. his location chief
    B. the general dispatcher
    C. the yard dispatcher
    D. the superintendent of operations

15. Following are four statements which might be correct concerning the use of extra lists by the transit authority:   15._____
    I. An extra list will be posted daily at each depot.
    II. A regular bus operator, who is scheduled to work a particular day, is assigned on that day to work as an extra. In this case, he should be assigned to work from the extra list after all the extra operators have been assigned.
    III. When an extra operator is assigned a day in advance to a regular run, he will be allowed time for the run on the same basis as the regular operator who held the run.
    IV. When a regular run has become permanently open and no extra-list operator has indicated a preference for it, the run shall be assigned to the first man on the list.
    Which of the following choices lists ALL of the above statements that are CORRECT?

    A. I, III   B. I, IV   C. II, III   D. III, IV

16. When a bus pulls out of a depot in order to start service on its route, the employee having final responsibility for making sure that the hand brakes of the bus are not defective is   16._____

    A. a maintenance supervisor
    B. the last bus maintainer who worked on the bus
    C. the bus operator
    D. the yard dispatcher

17. A bus line has 10 regular runs.   17._____
    The MINIMUM number of regular runs that must be open on this line before a pick is required to be held is

    A. 5   B. 4   C. 2   D. 1

18. On a particular bus route, the one-way running time is 50 minutes, and the layover time at each terminal is 6 minutes.   18._____
    If the headway is 7 minutes, then the number of buses required on this route is

    A. 8   B. 14   C. 16   D. 18

19. A passenger tells you that he fell on a bus as a result of the bus driver's poor driving ability and he wants to know how to file a claim for his injuries against the transit authority. The PROPER procedure for you to follow is to tell the passenger

    A. to give you his name and address and that a representative of the transit authority claims bureau will contact him
    B. that you are not permitted to give him any information
    C. to write to or personally visit the transit authority claims bureau
    D. that he will probably not be able to collect damages for that type of accident

20. During a snow emergency, a bus operator is ordered to call his depot, but is NOT ordered to report there in person.
    The amount of pay, at his regular rate, that he is entitled to for each required call to the depot is _____ hour's(hours') pay.

    A. 1   B. 1 1/2   C. 2   D. 2 1/2

---

## KEY (CORRECT ANSWERS)

| | | | |
|---|---|---|---|
| 1. | C | 11. | A |
| 2. | D | 12. | C |
| 3. | B | 13. | B |
| 4. | D | 14. | A |
| 5. | B | 15. | A |
| 6. | B | 16. | C |
| 7. | A | 17. | C |
| 8. | C | 18. | C |
| 9. | B | 19. | C |
| 10. | C | 20. | B |

# TEST 2

DIRECTIONS: Each question or incomplete statement is followed by several suggested answers or completions. Select the one that BEST answers the question or completes the statement. *PRINT THE LETTER OF THE CORRECT ANSWER IN THE SPACE AT THE RIGHT.*

1. According to the schedule of working conditions for bus operators, the percent of regular runs that are straight runs should be AT LEAST  1.____

   A. 50%    B. 55%    C. 60%    D. 65%

2. A bus operator who completes an additional 9 hours of emergency work after he has completed his regularly scheduled tour of duty should be paid a meal allowance of  2.____

   A. $4.50    B. $5.00
   C. $5.75    D. more than $6.00

3. Immediately after completing his tour of duty, a bus operator is required to report to the torts department in connection with a bus accident which he witnessed. NOT including his run pay, the TOTAL amount of pay which this bus operator is entitled to for reporting to the torts department is _____ hours pay.  3.____

   A. 2    B. 3    C. 4    D. 5

4. A bus operator with a weekday run pulls out of the depot at 1:15 P.M., swings from 4:53 P.M. to 5:37 P.M., and is relieved at a relief point at 10:10 P.M. The travel allowance back to the depot is 13 minutes, and the headway allowance for this run is 15 minutes. Including all allowances, the pay for this run, in hours and minutes, is _____ hours and _____ minutes.  4.____

   A. 9; 32    B. 10; 5    C. 10; 27    D. 10; 35

5. When a fire drill occurs at a school and there is a line of children outside the school, a bus operator must NOT operate his bus within _____ feet from the line of children.  5.____

   A. 100    B. 150    C. 200    D. 250

6. A bus operator is unable to be present in person at a pick and has left a list of choices with his superior. If none of the operator's choices is available during the pick, his superior should  6.____

   A. contact the operator by telephone and request him to change his choices
   B. select and assign the operator to the earliest finishing run which he would be entitled to
   C. place the operator's name at the top of the extra list
   D. change the operator's pick time so that he can be present

7. When charges are brought against a bus operator, a copy of the charges from the assistant general superintendent is USUALLY presented to the operator by the  7.____

   A. location chief
   B. superintendent of operations
   C. crew dispatcher
   D. desk dispatcher

8. When a bus operator is required to appear in court, a record showing the date, time, and place of the appearance must be made in the *Court Book* by the

   A. crew dispatcher
   B. desk dispatcher
   C. location chief
   D. yard dispatcher

9. The one-way running time on a bus route is 1 hour and 6 minutes, and the average speed of a bus on this route is 14 MHP.
   What is the length of this route?
   _____ miles.

   A. 13.5   B. 14.0   C. 14.4   D. 15.4

10. A recent bulletin order states, in part, the following: *Courtesy is a requirement of the operator's job. A kind word, a helping hand where necessary, and a pleasant smite will make for a better relationship with the passengers and will elicit their cooperation with the operator in the performance of his duties.*
    Which of the following is MOST in agreement with the above information given in the bulletin order?

    A. When a bus operator is courteous, he will do a better job.
    B. A bus operator must be courteous to passengers only when they are courteous to him.
    C. Passengers should be treated courteously even though a bus operator is not required to be courteous.
    D. When a bus operator is courteous to passengers, he will find that passengers will tend to cooperate with him.

11. A bus consumes 45 gallons of fuel after having traveled a distance of 328 miles. The number of miles per gallon of fuel that this bus gets, based on this information, is CLOSEST to

    A. 6.8   B. 7.3   C. 7.8   D. 8.3

12. A bus operator, who has a student operator with him on the first half of his run, pulls out of the depot on a Wednesday at 11:02 A.M., swings from 3:06 P.M. to 3:48 P.M., and pulls back into the depot at 7:02 P.M. Including all allowances, the pay for this run on this day, in hours and minutes, is _____ hours and minutes.

    A. 9; 30   B. 10; 0   C. 10; 20   D. 10; 30

13. Assume that you are writing a report to your location chief in which you recommend changing an existing standard operating procedure.
    Of the following, the MOST important information that you should include in this report is a(n)

    A. completely detailed description of the present procedure
    B. list of the names and titles of all surface transportation department employees affected by the changed procedure
    C. list of the reasons explaining why the changed procedure is superior to the procedure which is presently being followed
    D. index of reports and documents that tend to support your recommendations

3 (#2)

14. If the length of a particular bus route is 7.4 miles and the average speed of a certain bus on this route is 9 miles per hour, then the one-way running time for this bus is APPROXIMATELY _____ minutes.

   A. 41.8    B. 43.4    C. 46.2    D. 49.3

   14._____

15. An *extra run* is one that requires NO more than _____ hours work.

   A. 3    B. 4    C. 5    D. 6

   15._____

16. A bus operator with a weekday run whose hourly rate of pay is $12.60 normally reports for work at 7:30 A.M. and clears at 3:00 P.M.
   What is his GROSS pay for a day on which he is required to write an accident report at the end of his run?

   A. $107.10    B. $108.90    C. $113.40    D. $115.60

   16._____

17. Unless specifically directed otherwise, bus operators are required to shut off their bus engines while waiting at terminal stops in order to reduce air pollution. Failure to comply with this rule can subject an operator to a MINIMUM penalty of

   A. $100    B. $150    C. $200    D. $250

   17._____

18. When a line is discontinued, those bus operators losing runs will be placed on the extra list and arrangements must be made to hold a _____ pick.

   A. depot          B. line
   C. division       D. line or a depot

   18._____

19. A passenger count was made at a certain terminal between 8 A.M. and 9 A.M., and it was noted that eight buses were loaded with the following number of passengers: 34, 52, 29, 63, 19, 17, 56, and 42, respectively.
   The TOTAL number of passengers boarding these eight buses was

   A. 302    B. 312    C. 313    D. 412

   19._____

20. The code that a bus operator should use over the two-way radio when reporting a disabled bus is Code

   A. 3    B. 4    C. 5    D. 6

   20._____

## KEY (CORRECT ANSWERS)

1. A
2. D
3. D
4. B
5. A

6. B
7. A
8. A
9. D
10. D

11. B
12. C
13. C
14. D
15. D

16. A
17. D
18. A
19. B
20. A

# EXAMINATION SECTION
# TEST 1

DIRECTIONS: Each question or incomplete statement is followed by several suggested answers or completions. Select the one that BEST answers the question or completes the statement. *PRINT THE LETTER OF THE CORRECT ANSWER IN THE SPACE AT THE RIGHT.*

1. A certain bus operator reports for work on Monday at 9:00 A.M. and normally clears at 4:30 P.M. He is paid at the hourly rate of $12.80.
   What should his GROSS pay be for this day if due to unusually heavy traffic conditions he gets only 10 minutes for lunch?

   A. $114.00  B. $109.80  C. $108.80  D. $102.40

   1.____

2. On the dispatcher's daily report of intervals operated and passenger traffic checks, there are column headings for recording each of the following EXCEPT

   A. run numbers
   B. route numbers
   C. passenger counts
   D. names of bus operators

   2.____

3. On the daily trip report, the code letter *A* is used to indicate

   A. extra trips (scheduled or unscheduled)
   B. late pull-in
   C. turned short of scheduled destination
   D. scheduled one-way trips lost

   3.____

4. When a bus operator is required to report to the medical staff for a physical examination outside his tour of duty, he will be paid at his regular rate for_____ hour(s).

   A. 1  B. 2  C. 3  D. 4

   4.____

5. Following are four statements concerning the operation of buses which might be correct:
   I. Operators of buses must exercise such control as to preclude the possibility of more than two buses entering or standing in a bus stop simultaneous
   II. Where flood conditions exist, bus operators must not operate through the water even at a slow rate of speed
   III. Bus operators must operate their buses in accordance with their schedule at all times
   IV. In no case should a bus operator use a bus to push other buses or vehicles
   Which of the following choices lists all of the above statements that are correct and none that is incorrect?

   A. I  B. I, II  C. III  D. III, IV

   5.____

Questions 6-9.

DIRECTIONS: Questions 6 through 9 are based on the bulletin order shown below titled TRESPASSERS ON TRANSIT AUTHORITY SURFACE PROPERTIES. Refer to this bulletin order when answering these questions.

## TRESPASSERS ON TRANSIT AUTHORITY SURFACE PROPERTIES

*Your attention is again directed to the need for rigid controls . to prevent unauthorized persons from entering Transit Authority property.*

*All strangers or persons who are not recognized as having official business on the property will be questioned by the first member of supervision who encounters them and such persons will be ejected immediately upon failure to present authorization or valid reason for being on the property.*

*In all cases where trespassers refuse to leave the property, or offer physical resistance to ejection, the Transit Authority police will be promptly notified for assistance and all members of supervision present will assist in the immediate identification and ejection of the trespassers.*
*Where property protection employees are assigned, they too will be notified.*

*Immediately following the call for Transit police assistance, notice of the circumstances will be given to surface control on Extension B6-504.*

*All surface transportation employees must be advised that entrance and exit from surface properties must be through authorized locations only, and failure to comply will be considered a flagrant disregard for outstanding regulations.*

*Finally, a complete written report is to be forwarded to the Assistant General Superintendent, Operations, of all instances dealing with the above.*

6. The following are four possible cases that might be correct in which a supervisor may eject a person whom he does not recognize from Transit Authority property: The person
    I. has a legitimate reason for being on Transit Authority property
    II. presents authorization for being on Transit Authority property
    III. has accidently wandered onto Transit Authority property
    IV. has no proof of his identity
   Which of the following choices lists all of the above cases that are CORRECT?

   A. I, II      B. I, III      C. II, IV      D. III, IV

7. If a supervisor is uncertain that a person who he does NOT know has official business on Transit Authority property, the FIRST action that the supervisor should take is to

   A. eject the person
   B. call the Transit Authority police
   C. call other members of supervision for assistance
   D. question the person

8. When an unauthorized person has been ejected from Transit Authority property, a written report of the incident must be forwarded to

   A. the Superintendent of Operations
   B. Surface Control
   C. the Assistant General Superintendent, Operations
   D. the location chief

9. The following are four possible situations that might be correct in which the Transit Authority police should be notified for assistance:
   I. A trespasser refuses to leave Transit Authority property
   II. A trespasser is encountered on Transit Authority property
   III. A stranger enters Transit Authority property through an unauthorized entrance
   IV. A trespasser physically resists ejection

   Which of the following choices lists all of the above situations that are CORRECT?

   A. I, III    B. I, IV    C. II, III    D. III, IV

10. When a general dispatcher assigns a code classification of C for an accident, it indicates that the degree of responsibility for the bus operator involved in the accident is

    A. 25%    B. 50%    C. 75%    D. 100%

11. When a special inspector requests information from a bus operator, the inspector is required to identify himself by showing the operator

    A. a special identification card
    B. his badge
    C. both a special identification card and his badge
    D. a letter authorizing his request for information

12. A situation arises and you find that you must criticize a bus operator for poor work performance.
    Of the following, it is MOST important for you to

    A. inform the operator about his grievance rights
    B. obtain approval of your action from your supervisor
    C. keep a record of what you say to the operator
    D. be specific about your criticism and not to use generalities

13. When two bus operators want to exchange runs permanently after schedules are picked, the exchange must be approved by the

    A. assistant general superintendent
    B. superintendent of operations
    C. location chief
    D. crew dispatcher

14. A bus operator reports on a Monday at 2:09 A.M., swings from 5:32 A.M. to 6:16 A.M., and clears at 10:21 A.M.
    The night differential for this run, in hours and minutes, is ____ hours and ____ minutes.

    A. 8; 12    B. 3; 50    C. 3; 23    D. 0; 0

15. The run pay, in hours and minutes, for a bus operator who reports on a weekday at 11:42 M., swings from 3:29 P.M. to 4:17 P.M., and clears at 9:08 P.M. is ____ hours and ____ minutes.

    A. 10; 9    B. 9; 45    C. 9; 23    D. 8; 0

16. The code that is used over the two-way radio for messages pertaining to winter operations, such as reporting snow drifts, is code 16.___

    A. 9  B. 10  C. 11  D. 12

17. Bus operators who qualify to receive 60% sick pay may receive this benefit if they are out sick for a MINIMUM of _____ or more consecutive working days. 17.___

    A. 5  B. 9  C. 14  D. 21

18. When a dispatcher makes it a practice to be fair and firm in disciplining bus operators in all cases of rule violations, including those of a minor nature, it is considered a 18.___

    A. *good* practice, because it makes it easier for the dispatcher to administer discipline on this basis
    B. *bad* practice, because employees do not want to be disciplined for minor violations
    C. *good* practice, because not administering discipline for minor violations can lead to a more serious erosion of discipline
    D. *bad* practice, since administering discipline for minor violations leads to union complaints

19. After the commencement of operations of a new line, all runs on the new line must be put up for a depot pick WITHIN 19.___

    A. 48 hours  B. 3 days  C. 5 days  D. 2 weeks

20. Of the following, the BEST course of action for a dispatcher to follow when he observes for the first time a bus operator scraping the tires of his bus against the curb is to 20.___

    A. observe the operator to see whether he commits other driving mistakes
    B. inform the operator of the mistake he made and observe whether he makes this same driving mistake in the future
    C. reprimand the operator and warn him that you will be watching him closely
    D. make a record of the occurrence and bring it to the attention of the location chief

# KEY (CORRECT ANSWERS)

| | | | |
|---|---|---|---|
| 1. | C | 11. | A |
| 2. | D | 12. | D |
| 3. | D | 13. | A |
| 4. | C | 14. | B |
| 5. | A | 15. | B |
| 6. | D | 16. | C |
| 7. | D | 17. | B |
| 8. | C | 18. | C |
| 9. | B | 19. | A |
| 10. | B | 20. | B |

# TEST 2

DIRECTIONS: Each question or incomplete statement is followed by several suggested answers or completions. Select the one that BEST answers the question or completes the statement. *PRINT THE LETTER OF THE CORRECT ANSWER IN THE SPACE AT THE RIGHT.*

Questions 1-12.

DIRECTIONS: Questions 1 through 12 are based on the partly filled-in schedule shown on the next page..

1. The TOTAL PAY for Run No. 27, in hours and minutes, is
   A. 8:00   B. 8:53   C. 8:55   D. 9:20

   1.____

2. Of the following runs, the one which has the most TRAVEL time is Run No.
   A. 26   B. 29   C. 30   D. 31

   2.____

3. The paid SWING for Run No. 28, in minutes, is
   A. 0   B. 52   C. 56   D. 60

   3.____

4. The total TRAVEL time for Run No. 27, in minutes, is
   A. 5   B. 10   C. 15   D. 20

   4.____

5. The overtime ALLOWANCE for Run No. 28, in minutes, is
   A. 0   B. 5   C. 9   D. 14

   5.____

6. The TOTAL PAY for Run No. 30, in hours and minutes, is
   A. 7:14   B. 8:00   C. 8:02   D. 8:03

   6.____

7. For Run No. 29, the total number of TRIPS, including any trips made going to and from the depot, for both halves of the run is
   A. 4   B. 7   C. 8   D. 9

   7.____

8. The SPREAD for Run No. 29, in hours and minutes, is
   A. 7:07   B. 7:18   C. 7:23   D. 7:43

   8.____

9. The total MILEAGE accumulated for all six runs shown on the schedule is
   A. 330   B. 339   C. 340   D. 350

   9.____

10. The VEHICLE time for Run No. 30, in hours and minutes, is
    A. 6:49   B. 7:14   C. 7:19   D. 7:37

    10.____

11. The BOOST time for Run No. 26, in minutes, is
    A. 0   B. 7   C. 17   D. 59

    11.____

12. For Run No. 27, the total number of TRIPS, including any trips made going to and from the depot, for the first half of the run is
    A. 4   B. 5   C. 6   D. 7

    12.____

USE THIS SCHEDULE FOR ANSWERING QUESTIONS 1 TO 12

ROUTE: B - 909 - APPLE ST.     BROOKLYN DIVISION

WEEKDAY SCHEDULE MO. S - 305

EFFECTIVE: APRIL 26     EAST NEW TOWN DEPOT

| Run | Re-port | A.M. | P.O. | | | | | | | | | | | | mileage | Clear | TIME-HOURS & MINUTES / PAY TIME |
|---|---|---|---|---|---|---|---|---|---|---|---|---|---|---|---|---|---|
| 26 | A.M. 916 | P.O. 926 | 936 1041 | 1142 1247 | 158 - | 207 R-22 | | W 259 R-7 | - 359 | 454 R-40 | | | | | 39 19 | 509 | |
| 27 | A.M. 921 | | R-7 | 936 | 955 1102 | 1214 119 | T 222 - | 227 R-44 | | | 322 R-21 | 334 429 | 550 - | 559 R-47 | 38 24 | 614 | |
| 28 | A.M. 928 | | R-4 | 943 | 1006 1111 | 1214 119 | 230 - | 239 R-35 | | | 335 R-14 | - 431 | 552 R-43 | | 39 18 | 537 | |
| 29 | A.M. 930 | P.O. 940 | 945 1052 | 1206 | 1215 R-18 | | | W 1251 R-3 | - 151 | 302 407 | 458 R-41 | | | | 23 35 | 513 | |
| 30 | A.M. 936 | P.O. 946 | 956 1101 | 1206 111 | 222 - | 231 R-23 | | | 319 R-8 | - 415 | T 518 - | 523 R-66 | | | 39 20 | 538 | |
| 31 | A.M. 1008 | R-10 | 1023 | - 1119 | 1222 127 | 222 R-25 | | W 315 R-33 | - 415 | 526 - | 535 R-67 | | | | 34 22 | 550 | |

SYMBOLS:
PLAIN TRIPS - Lemon St. and Orange St. to Apple St. and Oak St.
T TRIPS - Peach St. and Apple St. to Elm St.
W TRIPS - Lemon St. and Orange St. to 11m St.

NOTES:
FROM: Lemon St. and Orange St. via Orange St. and Apple St. to Oak St.
RETURN: Via Apple St. and Orange St. to Lemon St.
RELIEFS MADE AT CHERRY ST. AND APPLE ST. 3 5 MINUTE TRAVEL ALLOWANCE, VIA ROUTE B-816

13. Supervisors should see to it that personal calls made by employees over the transit authority telephone system are reduced to the barest minimum PRIMARILY because

    A. these calls interfere with essential transit authority business
    B. allowing employees to make too many personal calls may cause a reduction in morale
    C. these calls usually involve emergencies which can affect an employee's performance
    D. these calls deprive the telephone company of revenue in their public telephones on transit authority property

14. When a dispatcher gives instructions to a bus operator, the dispatcher will MOST likely avoid confusing the operator if

    A. he gives the instructions to the operator as quickly as possible
    B. he repeats the instructions to the operator several times using different words each time
    C. his instructions are clear and concise
    D. his instructions contain as many details as possible

15. A recent bulletin order cautions bus operators NOT to operate close to burning flares marking traffic hazards. Following are four possible reasons for this caution which may be correct:
    I. The transit authority must pay for the cost of replacing damaged flares
    II. The bus equipment can be damaged
    III. The effectiveness of these flares may be impaired
    IV. Operating closer than 10 feet from a burning flare constitutes a traffic violation

    Which of the following choices lists all of the above reasons that are CORRECT according to the bulletin order?

    A. I, II        B. I, III        C. II, III        D. III, IV

16. The patrol car log is used by patrol car dispatchers to keep a record of

    A. violations issued
    B. schedule changes
    C. maintenance performed on the patrol car
    D. radio messages received in the patrol car

17. A bus operator finishes his regular run and is then assigned a second piece of work. He will be paid time and one-half for reserve time, provided the difference between the clearing time of the first piece and the reporting time of the second piece of work does NOT exceed

    A. 30 minutes        B. 45 minutes
    C. 59 minutes        D. 2 hours

18. On a particular bus line, 10 buses per hour are scheduled to leave a terminal between the hours of 4:00 P.M. and 6:00 P.M., while 6 buses per hour are scheduled to leave between 6:00 P.M. and 8:00 P.M.
    The increase in headway after 6:00 P.M. is CLOSEST to _____ minutes.

    A. 10   B. 8   C. 6   D. 4

19. According to step 1 of the grievance procedure, a bus operator may present a grievance to his immediate superior

    A. in writing personally only
    B. orally only
    C. orally, or in writing personally only
    D. orally, or in writing personally, or through the union

20. According to the grievance procedure, after an aggrieved bus operator has received an unfavorable step 2 decision, he nay appeal this decision, but must do so within _____ days.

    A. 2   B. 3   C. 4   D. 5

# KEY (CORRECT ANSWERS)

1. B
2. D
3. C
4. B
5. A

6. C
7. C
8. D
9. D
10. A

11. B
12. C
13. A
14. C
15. C

16. D
17. C
18. D
19. D
20. B

# EXAMINATION SECTION
# TEST 1

DIRECTIONS: Each question or incomplete statement is followed by several suggested answers or completions. Select the one that BEST answers the question or completes the statement. *PRINT THE LETTER OF THE CORRECT ANSWER IN THE SPACE AT THE RIGHT.*

1. The MOST effective approach a senior surface line dispatcher can pursue in verbally transmitting a controversial order to his subordinates is to

    A. state the order and promptly hold an open discussion with his subordinates on it
    B. make a simple statement of the order without commenting on it
    C. state the order and forbid his subordinates to discuss it while on duty
    D. state the order and briefly justify the controversial parts

2. A surface line operator scheduled to work on Labor Day was reported sick by his wife three hours before his reporting time, and a substitute was found to work his tour. According to the rules, the operator reported sick

    A. is charged with two days of unpaid sick leave
    B. has his choice of receiving holiday pay or being credited with one day of sick leave
    C. loses his holiday pay and any compensatory time off in lieu of the holiday
    D. retains his right to have another day off in lieu of the holiday but loses his holiday pay

3. The one of the following which is NOT required to properly identify a letter-carrier entitled to free transportation on surface lines where such free transportation is provided is the letter-carrier's

    A. regulation bag            B. uniform cap
    C. regulation badge          D. uniform

4. In a recent bulletin, operators were warned that summonses would be issued to those who left their engines running for more than three minutes while standing at a terminal, that they themselves would have to pay any fines assessed in consequence of such summonses, and that departmental charges would be preferred against offenders. The reason for the threatened severity of punishment is to impress on operators the necessity for reduction of

    A. complaints from local residents
    B. complaints from passengers
    C. noise
    D. air pollution

5. A certain bus route is five miles long. The schedule speed for half of the route is 6 M.P.H., and for the other half of the route it is 15 M.P.H. The average schedule speed for the *ENTIRE* route

    A. is between 6 M.P.H. and 10.5 M.P.H.
    B. is exactly 10.5 M.P.H.
    C. is between 10.5 M.P.H. and 15 M.P.H.
    D. cannot be calculated without knowing running time for each half of the route

6. A dispatcher ordered an operator to move a bus through a narrow space in a depot, but the operator claimed that there was not sufficient clearance and refused to make the move. If this situation were referred to you, your PROPER action as depot supervisor would be to

   A. tell the operator to follow the dispatcher's order, but to move the bus slowly and cautiously
   B. direct the dispatcher to cite the operator for insubordination
   C. go to the location yourself and determine by inspection what ought to be done
   D. send for the instructor of operators and have him decide who is right

7. With respect to the issuance and collection of free transfers, it is MOST PROBABLY true that operators as a whole

   A. issue more on holidays than on ordinary weekdays
   B. issue more on any one day than they collect that same day
   C. collect more on short runs than on long runs
   D. collect more before noon than after noon on any day

8. With respect to the morale of employees, it is MOST GENERALLY agreed that morale is highest when employees have

   A. the highest wage rates in the industry
   B. the greatest latitude with respect to time off, coffee-breaks, etc.
   C. full confidence in management and supervision
   D. easy going supervisors who overlook most deviations from rules and regulations

9. A regular tour of duty for an operator requires him to report at 5:50 a.m., leave on his first run at 6:05 a.m., swing from 10:30 a.m. to 2:00 p.m., complete his last run at 5:10 p.m., and clear at 5:20 p.m. The normal pay for this tour is at the operator's regular rate for

   A. 9 hours, 30 min.  B. 9 hours, 45 min.
   C. 10 hours, 15 min.  D. 11 hours, 30 min.

10. An employee who has a wrist watch which gains 30 minutes per day sets it to the correct time at 6:00 a.m. When the watch indicates 12:00 noon, the CORRECT time to the nearest minute is

    A. 11:46  B. 11:53
    C. 12:07  D. 12:14

11. At about 5:30 p.m. on a weekday, the fare box on a certain bus stopped functioning. The bus route involved is from a subway station to an outlying residential area, and the fare box breakdown occurred a few streets after the start of the run. The procedure which you would approve would be to

    A. complete the regular run to the other terminus, making stops only to discharge passengers
    B. transfer the passengers to the next bus, and wait at the point of breakdown for a maintainer
    C. continue normal operation to the other terminus, and collect any addditional fares by hand
    D. return to the subway station, discharge passengers, and refund their fares

12. According to regulations, an operator whose vacation period includes both Veteran's Day and Thanksgiving Day, and who makes no other election in advance, will be compensated by

    A. having his vacation period extended two days
    B. being credited with two A.V.A. days
    C. being credited with an A.V.A. day and receiving eight hours extra pay
    D. receiving sixteen hours extra pay

13. If a senior surface line dispatcher finds that he has made a mistake in the details of a bulletin order issued to operators, the POOREST procedure for him to follow would be to

    A. depend on the natural alertness of employees to find the mistake and overcome it
    B. have the dispatchers correct it verbally
    C. issue individual correction slips to each employee
    D. issue a bulletin correcting the error

14. For pick purposes, a night trick (hawk) is classed as the next day's work if it starts at any time between certain specified limits. These limits are

    A. 9:30 p.m. and 11:59 p.m.
    B. 10:00 p.m. and 11:59 p.m.
    C. 10:30 p.m. and 11:59 p.m.
    D. 11:00 p.m. and 11:59 p.m.

15. It would be POOR policy for a senior surface line dispatcher to discuss with his subordinates the

    A. authority rules and regulations
    B. candidates in the mayoralty campaign
    C. maintenance of cleaner depot quarters
    D. job security policy of private bus companies

16. After a senior surface line dispatcher has criticized one of his subordinates for making a mistake, it would be BEST to

    A. remind the subordinate of his error from time to time in order to keep him on his toes
    B. impress the subordinate with the fact that he will be closely checked from then on
    C. suspend final judgment of the subordinate pending future performance
    D. overlook the next error in order to avoid any possible semblance of discrimination

17. According to official regulations, an operator must not use his bus to push another bus unless

    A. ordered to do so by a police officer
    B. he first investigates and it is to his satisfaction that passengers are fully protected from any possible injury
    C. the passengers are first removed from both buses
    D. ordered to do so by a member of the supervisory force

18. In the latest instructions for coping with the situation when one of a pair of rear dual tires on his bus becomes deflated, the operator is told to

    A. study the situation, then take the safe course
    B. stop immediatley and telephone headquarters for instructions
    C. discharge all passengers at the nearest bus stop and take the bus out of service
    D. complete his trip to the terminus and report the condition

19. Of the following conditions, the one which would be LEAST likely to cause a bus to be taken out of service is:

    A. Low hydraulic brake fluid which would require "pumping" of the brake pedal
    B. Defective wiring which results in the bus headlights switch being effective in the parking position only
    C. Failure of the bus heating system when the outside temperature is above 40
    D. Broken glass in the window alongside the bus operator

20. Considering only the following cases, the one that is likely to result in the SMALLEST penalty against an operator is:

    A. Reporting for duty under the influence of alcohol
    B. Absenting himself from duty several times without prior notification
    C. Depositing the fares in the fare box and returning the correct remaining change to all passengers not having exact fare
    D. Sustaining damage to his bus which was hit from the rear by a passenger car

21. When trolley coach operation is resumed after a complete stoppage (such as at 11:00 a.m. on Veteran's Day), operators are required to follow a prescribed procedure and to maintain a reduced speed for five minutes after the resumption of operation. The *PROBABLE* reason for these requirements is to PREVENT

    A. irregularity in schedules
    B. overcrowding at coach stops
    C. overloading electrical feeders
    D. damage to coach electrical equipment

22. Prompt operation of the tilt tray and counting mechanism of the fare box is required of bus operators. One good reason for requiring such prompt operation is that it

    A. reduces the possibilities of fare box defects due to imposing heavy loads on the mechanism
    B. prevents the deposit of spurious coins in the fare box
    C. reduces the temptation to potential thieves
    D. prevents loss of money when transferring coins from the fare box to coin holder

23. In making application for Social Security coverage under a plan, it is *MOST* important for the employee involved to have

    A. voted in the Social Security referendum
    B. produced official proof of age
    C. obtained and submitted his Social Security number
    D. been in the department at least six quarters

24. Two buses were involved in an accident when Bus No. 1 was passing Bus No. 2. Bus No. 1 was struck on the right side to the rear of the exit doors by Bus No. 2 which was starting out from a bus stop. In investigating this accident for the purpose of fixing responsibility, it would be LEAST important to determine whether the operator of

    A. Bus No. 1 sounded his horn
    B. Bus No. 2 was behind schedule
    C. Bus No. 1 reduced speed for passing
    D. Bus No. 2 signaled his intention of leaving the bus stop

24._____

25. It has been customary to permit the transfer of operators between the various divisions. In reference to such transfers, a TRUE statement is that:

    A. Written requests for transfers between divisions are accepted only at the time of the regular pick
    B. Operators accepting transfer to other divisions are placed at the bottom of the seniority list in the division to which they transfer, with permanent operators having preference status over temporary or provisional employees
    C. The integrated list of operators requesting transfer to another division is arranged in seniority preference order according to their original position on the Civil Service list
    D. It is understood that any employee transferred must be qualified for the job, and, in addition, must be able to meet the schedule within five (5) days

25._____

26. Of the following, it is LEAST important for an outside dispatcher at a fixed location to know the

    A. exact routing of all of the lines under his supervision
    B. names and pass numbers of the operators on the various lines under his supervision
    C. scheduled running times of the various lines passing his location
    D. headways in use on the different lines under his supervision

26._____

27. Although operators on duty are prohibited from going into restaurants for the purpose of obtaining food or drink, they may enter restaurants for personal necessities. One of your operators has been reported as making three stops at a certain restaurant during his tour of duty. In this case, your BEST course of action as senior surface line dispatcher would be to

    A. discuss the matter with the operator
    B. transmit this information to your superior
    C. assign a patrol car to further check on the operator
    D. telephone the restaurant to find out why the operator stops there so often

27._____

28. When system picks for operators' tours and tricks are held, the copy of the rules governing the pick given to each operator individually includes a

    A. list of operators in order of pick seniority
    B. statement of the date and time the operator is to pick
    C. description of each tour and trick to be picked
    D. statement of the amount of extra time allowed for picking

28._____

29. General operating practice is not to carry passengers on run-on or run-off trips. The MOST PROBABLE of the following possible reasons for this practice is that

    A. the law restricts the carrying of passengers on them
    B. it simplifies the schedules of inspection and repair
    C. very few people would be benefitted thereby
    D. operators would otherwise have to get paid overtime

30. Of the following, the MOST important duty of an outside dispatcher supervising the operation of buses in passenger service is to

    A. be constantly alert to prevent accidents
    B. reroute buses in emergencies
    C. investigate bus delays
    D. maintain a uniform headway

31. After discharging passengers at terminals, operators are required by current instructions to make their vehicles available for intending passengers

    A. as soon as they reach proper position in stand
    B. as soon as they have inspected the interior and picked up lost articles and large pieces of litter
    C. five minutes before scheduled departure time
    D. when all the seats in the preceding bus are occupied

32. According to the schedule of working conditions for operators, the one of the following statements concerning swing runs which is NOT true is that

    A. no part of the swing period shall be considered in computing overtime
    B. operators will be paid for any swing time in excess of two hours
    C. not more than one swing period is allowed in any one tour of duty
    D. the swing period must not be less than one hour nor more than two hours

33. From the standpoint of maintaining schedules with minimum fatigue to operators, it is LEAST important for buses in congested city service to have

    A. rear exit doors            B. power steering
    C. automatic transmission     D. high cruising speeds

34. The impact of the State motor vehicle financial security law on bus operators is that

    A. each operator must carry his own public liability insurance
    B. liability insurance cannot be obtained on buses unless operators can show financial responsibility
    C. driving an uninsured vehicle off the job may result in an operator's loss of his job
    D. bonding cannot be obtained for an operator unless he carries liability insurance

35. A published set of statistics in a certain year show that, of the automobile drivers involved in fatal accidents, 1.1% had less than 3 months of operating experience, 0.8% had between 3 and 6 months, 1.4% had between 6 and 12 months, and 96.7% had 1 year or more of operating experience. An ENTIRELY CORRECT statement which can be based upon these statistics alone is that

A. the more experience a driver had, the more likely he was to be involved in a fatal accident
B. the safest drivers were those having between 3 and 6 months of operating experience
C. most drivers involved in fatal accidents had a year or more of operating experience
D. more than 90% of fatal accidents involved drivers having just over a year of operating experience

36. The actual task of operating buses on schedule rests PRIMARILY on the

    A. fixed-location outside dispatchers
    B. patrolling outside dispatchers
    C. depot chiefs
    D. surface line operators

37. Assume that you instruct a dispatcher to improvise schedules based on a ten-minute headway leaving his terminal to cover a three-hour period during which the regularly scheduled headway is now twelve minutes.
If the terminal-to-terminal running time is exactly one hour and fifteen buses are normally in operation on the line during the three-hour period involved, the BEST operating practice would be to maintain the adjusted service with

    A. no extra buses            B. one extra bus
    C. two extra buses           D. three extra buses

38. The MOST ACCEPTABLE of the following statements concerning bus driving is that

    A. buses should be given the right-of-way over private cars
    B. operators should be permitted to pass red traffic lights when there is no cross traffic approaching
    C. operators should be more concerned with the welfare of their passengers than with themselves
    D. improved bus construction makes driving care less necessary than five years ago

39. Of the following items, the one LEAST important to a surface line operator in the daily performance of his duties is

    A. knowing the locations of time points
    B. knowledge of the schedule of working conditions
    C. knowledge of operating rules
    D. judgment of speed and distance

40. An operator who works a "special" for an hour-and-a-half after completing his regular tour which pays 8 hours, will receive extra pay for the "special" at his regular rate for

    A. 2 hours      B. 2 1/4 hours      C. 3 hours      D. 4 hours

41. Since the bus operator is the authority's most frequent direct contact with the public, it is MOST important in the interest of good public relations to impress on operators the necessity of

    A. starting out slowly from bus stops
    B. keeping their buses free of litter
    C. being patient and polite in dealing with passengers
    D. calling out the names of all streets as they approach them

8 (#1)

42. Assume that you have continually requested the assignment of more extra operators to your depot because you have been forced to resort to overtime to cover shortages, and that four extra operators have finally been transferred from another depot. When these men actually report, the CORRECT procedure will be to

    A. add their names to the bottom of the extra list
    B. hold a depot pick
    C. hold a line pick
    D. use them to fill permanently open regular runs

43. A traffic signal at an intersection may develop a defect resulting in the signal becoming dark. Instructions to operators on how to operate past such a dark signal would be BEST if they included the caution to operate as though the signal were a

    A. red light
    B. flashing yellow light
    C. yield-right-of-way sign
    D. stop sign

44. Assume that it is called to your attention that several operators clearing between 10:00 p.m. and midnight at your depot turned in used transfers dated the following day. Your CORRECT position in this regard should be that the

    A. procedure for the handling of transfers should be reviewed so that it can be seen whether or not the loopholes can be plugged
    B. operators issuing and accepting the transfers must be cautioned to be more alert
    C. occurrence is normal under the rules
    D. dispatcher responsible for issuing and collecting transfers must be cautioned against future slip-ups

45. In the course of making the rounds of your depot, you should take prompt action under the rules to stop an operator if he were

    A. eating his lunch while sitting in a bus in the garage
    B. filling out his daily report while sitting at a table in the garage
    C. closing the windows of a bus he had just parked in the garage
    D. backing a bus, with the aid of hand signals from a maintainer, from the street into the garage

46. If you were requested by your local civic association to address a meeting on the subject of bus transportation, it would be BEST for you to

    A. accept without reservation because it is an opportunity to clear up misunderstandings
    B. decline with regrets because you are not an official representative of the authority
    C. reserve your answer until you have reported the invitation to your department head and informed him of your desire to accept or decline
    D. withhold your answer until you have personally investigated as to whether anyone in the association has an "axe to grind"

47. A senior surface line dispatcher will, MOST LIKELY, secure the respect of his subordinates if he

    A. knows his job thoroughly
    B. is very friendly with them
    C. overlooks some of the minor rules
    D. insists on strictly formal relations

48. There is a rule that passengers riding free on the buses must not occupy seats if paying passengers are standing. A dispatcher should interpret this rule to mean that

    A. the authority's aim is to make bus transportation less attractive to free riders
    B. it is for effect only and cannot be enforced
    C. a bus operator should request a school child to surrender his seat to a paying passenger
    D. he should brief his operators on what to inform free passengers, when necessary, in reference to occupying seats

49. You are preparing a complete report for the department on a depot reorganization study which you have made. Of the following sections, the one which should appear FIRST in the report is the

    A. description of the procedure you followed in organizing and conducting the study
    B. type of organization used in other surface line systems
    C. summary of the conclusions you have come to as a result of the study
    D. tabulation of supporting statistics

50. A personal acquaintance who knows you are in charge of a depot claims that there are delays on his bus line every morning causing him to be late to work; he asks you to "look into the matter" for him and try to improve the service. Considering your official position, your BEST answer to the complaint is to tell him that

    A. you will look into the matter
    B. the authority does the best it can considering traffic conditions
    C. he should send a letter to the authority giving specific dates and times
    D. you don't believe a bus line can be delayed every morning, and he should try leaving home earlier

## KEY (CORRECT ANSWERS)

| | | | | |
|---|---|---|---|---|
| 1. D | 11. A | 21. C | 31. A | 41. C |
| 2. C | 12. D | 22. A | 32. D | 42. A |
| 3. D | 13. A | 23. C | 33. D | 43. D |
| 4. D | 14. B | 24. B | 34. C | 44. C |
| 5. A | 15. B | 25. B | 35. C | 45. A |
| 6. B | 16. C | 26. B | 36. D | 46. C |
| 7. B | 17. D | 27. A | 37. A | 47. A |
| 8. C | 18. D | 28. B | 38. C | 48. D |
| 9. B | 19. C | 29. C | 39. B | 49. C |
| 10. B | 20. D | 30. D | 40. D | 50. C |

# EXAMINATION SECTION
## TEST 1

DIRECTIONS: Each question or incomplete statement is followed by several suggested answers or completions. Select the one that BEST answers the question or completes the statement. *PRINT THE LETTER OF THE CORRECT ANSWER IN THE SPACE AT THE RIGHT.*

1. A bus line has 15 regular runs.
 The MINIMUM number of regular runs that must be open on this line before a line pick is required to be held is

 A. 1     B. 2     C. 3     D. 5

 1.____

2. When a code responsibility classification of *B* is assigned for an accident, it indicates that the degree of contributory negligence on the part of the operator is

 A. 75%     B. 50%     C. 25%     D. 0%

 2.____

3. If it takes a bus 30 seconds to pass two check points that are 500 feet apart, then the speed of the bus is APPROXIMATELY _____ mph.

 A. 10.1     B. 11.4     C. 12.7     D. 14.2

 3.____

4. When a trespasser is caught on surface transportation property, a complete written report must be prepared and finally forwarded to the

 A. transit authority police
 B. yard dispatcher
 C. superintendent of operations
 D. assistant general superintendent, surface transportation

 4.____

5. A capable supervisor should check all operations under his control.
 Of the following, the LEAST important reason for doing this is to make sure that

 A. operations are being performed as scheduled
 B. he personally observes all operations at all times
 C. all the operations are still needed
 D. his manpower is being utilized efficiently

 5.____

6. The Keene equipment at bus depots retrieves coins from buses PRIMARILY by means of a

 A. vacuum system
 B. mechanical conveyor
 C. hydraulic transfer mechanism
 D. magnetic system

 6.____

7. The door interlock switch on buses must be in the *ON* position

 A. only when deemed necessary by the bus operator
 B. only while the bus is moving
 C. at all times
 D. only when the bus is in passenger service

 7.____

8. If an experienced bus operator has a student operator assigned to him for 6 hours on a particular day, the experienced operator is entitled to an instruction allowance of _____ hours at his regular rate of pay.

   A. two   B. four   C. six   D. eight

9. The report covering inactive bus operators should be submitted to the assistant general superintendent on a _____ basis.

   A. daily   B. weekly   C. monthly   D. six-month

10. In preparing a manual of operations for bus operators, of the following, it would be LEAST essential to

    A. describe alternative methods other than those recommended
    B. be concise rather than wordy
    C. use ordinary vocabulary except where technical language is required
    D. use pictures to illustrate parts of the text

11. The run pay, in hours and minutes, for an operator who reports on a weekday at 10:20 A.M., swings from 12:50 A.M. to 1:20 P.M., and clears at 7:06 P.M. is

    A. 8:16   B. 8:24   C. 8:54   D. 9:09

12. A dispatcher who is usually responsible for handling paycheck shortages of bus operators at a depot is

    A. the crew dispatcher
    B. the yard dispatcher
    C. a senior surface line dispatcher
    D. the general dispatcher

13. Of the following, when a road dispatcher goes on duty, he is NOT required to have in his possession

    A. booking sheets
    B. violation sheets
    C. complete bus schedules for his routes
    D. recaps for his routes

14. When a bus has run an extra trip, the bus operator should enter on the daily trip report the code letter

    A. A   B. B   C. C   D. D

15. A bus operator was assigned to emergency work after completion of his regularly scheduled tour of duty. If the operator worked 8 hours of emergency work, he should be paid _____ meal allowance(s).

    A. 1   B. 2   C. 3   D. 4

16. An *Alert/General Orders* message concerning a hurricane weather forecast transmitted over the two-way radio system is classified as a Code

    A. 1   B. 4   C. 5   D. 10

17. In order to abide by the transit authority rules, a bus operator calling in sick must notify the crew dispatcher AT LEAST _____ hour(s) before his tour of duty.

    A. 1  B. 2  C. 3  D. 4

18. On a certain bus line, 12 buses per hour are scheduled to leave a terminal between 8:00 M. and 10:00 A.M., while 4 buses per hour are scheduled to leave between 10:00 A.M. and 1:00 P.M.
    The change in headway after 10:00 A.M. is CLOSEST to a(n) _____ minutes.

    A. increase of 15
    B. increase of 10
    C. decrease of 15
    D. decrease of 10

19. When an operator is involved in an accident, it is necessary to fill out a Department of Motor Vehicles Accident form, MV-104.
    A copy of the completed form must be sent to each of the following EXCEPT

    A. Albany
    B. the assistant general superintendent, surface transportation
    C. the transit authority legal department
    D. the operator's depot file

20. When the *A/C STOP* tell-tale light is lit on a bus, it indicates that the air

    A. operated service brakes are applied
    B. pressure is low
    C. operated doors are not operating properly
    D. conditioner is not operating properly

21. The function of the brake interlock on buses is to

    A. set the proper idling speed
    B. prevent the engine from exceeding idling speed when the rear doors are open
    C. set the top speed of the engines
    D. apply the rear brakes when the rear doors are open

22. The FIRST action that a supervisor should take when he observes a stranger on surface transportation property is to

    A. ask him to leave
    B. call the transit authority police
    C. question the person on his reason for being there
    D. notify the radio operations center

23. The FS-20 field strength meter is used to check

    A. a defective bus radio
    B. the field of vision of a bus operator
    C. the state of charge of a bus battery
    D. the output of a bus generator

24. When a bus operator having a regular run is on jury duty, he is entitled to receive for each day of jury duty

   A. 8 hours pay
   B. division pay
   C. run pay and any night differential due him
   D. depot pay and any night differential due him

25. A bus operator reports on a weekday at 1:08 A.M., swings from 5:53 A.M. to 6:41 A.M., and clears at 9:27 A.M. The pay for this run, in hours and minutes, is

   A. 8:19 and a night differential of 4:51
   B. 8:29 and a night differential of 4:52
   C. 8:41 and a night differential of 8:19
   D. 8:00 and no night differential

26. Two bus operators at a depot want to temporarily exchange runs for a period of one week.
   The LOWEST level official from whom they may obtain permission to do this is the

   A. superintendent of operations
   B. location chief
   C. assistant general superintendent
   D. general dispatcher

27. Each of the two surface transportation divisions consists of _____ depots.

   A. 4    B. 5    C. 6    D. 7

28. Code 3 for the two-way surface transportation radio system is used in connection with

   A. winter operations        B. a collision
   C. a disabled bus           D. a blocked bus

29. Bus headways are split PRIMARILY because

   A. of bad weather conditions
   B. an operator has to make an extra run
   C. a regular run has been omitted
   D. a schedule contains too many short runs

30. When a bus operator pulls a bus out of a depot or yard for passenger service, he must make an operating test of the hand brakes.
    Unless otherwise designated, the hand brakes should be tested by the operator

   A. at a point approaching the building line exit doors of depots and yards
   B. at the place where he initially boards the bus
   C. immediately after he pulls out of the depot or yard
   D. just prior to the point at which he runs onto his route

31. When a bus approaches a railroad crossing, the operator must make a full stop a certain distance from the nearest rail of the railroad crossing.
    This distance should be _____ feet from the nearest rail.

   A. more than 75        B. not more than 75
   C. more than 50        D. not more than 50

32. When a bus operator who has no boost time in his run pay is required to remain at a depot to prepare an accident report, he should be paid  32.____

   A. for the exact amount of time required to fill out the report
   B. one hour's pay at his regular rate
   C. a boost of one-half hour
   D. two hours' pay at his regular rate

33. If the length of a particular bus route is 8.6 miles and the average speed of a bus on this route is 7.5 miles per hour, then the one-way running time for a bus is _____ minutes.  33.____

   A. 52.3　　　　B. 64.5　　　　C. 68.8　　　　D. 75.6

Questions 34-40.

DIRECTIONS: Questions 34 through 40 are based on the sample schedule shown below. Refer to this schedule when answering these questions. Assume that all operations proceed as scheduled unless otherwise stated in the question.

ROGER DEPOT

ROUTE: A-4 Logan Blvd.
WEEKDAY SCHEDULE NO.
BB-3 EFFECTIVE 1/1

| HEADWAYS | | | RUNNING TIME From Jane St. and from Carol St. | |
|---|---|---|---|---|
| From Jane St. and from Carol St. | | | 11:00 P.M. – 7:00 A.M. | 7:00 A.M. – 11:00 P.M. |
| 12:00 Mid. | - | Jane St. | - | - |
| 4:30 A.M. | 20 min. | George St. | 8 min. | 10 min. |
| 7:00 A.M. | 15 min. | Nick St. | 7 min. | 9 min. |
| 10:00 A.M. | 4 min. | Burt St. | 9 min. | 12 min. |
| 3:00 P.M. | 8 min. | Erica St. | 6 min. | 9 min. |
| 7:00 P.M. | 5 min. | Sam St. | 4 min. | 7 min. |
| 12:00 Mid. | 15 min. | Len St. | 11 min. | 13 min. |
| | | Tom St. | 5 min | 7 min. |
| | | Carol St. | 10 min. | 11 min. |
| | | | 60 min. | 78 min. |

SOUTHBOUND BUSES LEAVE FROM JANE ST.
NORTHBOUND BUSES LEAVE FROM CAROL ST.

34. The bus leaving Jane Street at 6:15 A.M. should arrive at Carol Street at _____ A.M.  34.____

   A. 7:15　　　　B. 7:18　　　　C. 7:24　　　　D. 7:33

35. The bus leaving Jane Street at 6:30 A.M. should arrive at Len Street at _____ A.M.  35.____

   A. 7:07　　　　B. 7:15　　　　C. 7:20　　　　D. 7:38

36. The buses leaving Jane Street at 6:30 A.M. and 6:45 A.M. should arrive at Carol Street _____ minutes apart.

    A. 15	B. 17	C. 19	D. 21

37. The southbound bus leaving Nick Street at 6:45 A.M. should arrive at Tom Street at _____ A.M.

    A. 7:20	B. 7:27	C. 7:38	D. 7:48

38. If the southbound bus leaving Jane Street at 6:30 A.M. is delayed for 6 minutes at Burt Street, it will then arrive at Tom Street at _____ A.M.

    A. 7:24	B. 7:36	C. 7:43	D. 7:46

39. If the layover time at Carol Street is 5 minutes, a bus leaving Jane Street at 5:45 A.M. should return to Jane Street at _____ A.M.

    A. 7:50	B. 7:55	C. 8:07	D. 8:12

40. If the distance from Jane Street to Carol Street is 14 miles, then the bus leaving Jane Street at 7:00 A.M. should be traveling at an average speed that is CLOSEST to _____ mph.

    A. 10.8	B. 12.2	C. 13	D. 14

# KEY (CORRECT ANSWERS)

| | | | |
|---|---|---|---|
| 1. B | 11. C | 21. D | 31. B |
| 2. C | 12. D | 22. C | 32. B |
| 3. B | 13. C | 23. A | 33. C |
| 4. D | 14. C | 24. C | 34. B |
| 5. B | 15. B | 25. A | 35. C |
| 6. A | 16. D | 26. B | 36. D |
| 7. C | 17. A | 27. B | 37. B |
| 8. A | 18. B | 28. C | 38. B |
| 9. C | 19. B | 29. C | 39. C |
| 10. A | 20. D | 30. A | 40. A |

# TEST 2

DIRECTIONS: Each question or incomplete statement is followed by several suggested answers or completions. Select the one that BEST answers the question or completes the statement. *PRINT THE LETTER OF THE CORRECT ANSWER IN THE SPACE AT THE RIGHT.*

1. The grievance procedure for surface line dispatchers consists of _____ steps.  1._____

    A. 2  B. 3  C. 4  D. 5

2. Assume that you have been assigned the task of simplifying the reports used by general dispatchers.  2._____
In order to accomplish this task successfully, of the following, one of the BEST procedures for you to follow is to

    A. avoid taking into consideration any complex features of the present reports
    B. assign a general dispatcher to the job, instructing him to disregard all aspects of the present reports
    C. request a number of experienced general dispatchers to submit suggestions of their own
    D. assign an inexperienced general dispatcher to work on this task allowing him to take as much time as necessary

3. If it becomes necessary to criticize a subordinate for poor work performance, it is MOST important for the supervisor to  3._____

    A. threaten the employee with severe disciplinary action
    B. criticize him in the presence of others
    C. be specific about his criticism and not to use generalities
    D. point out to the employee his past mistakes

4. When a subordinate has done a very good job in completing a difficult assignment, it would be MOST appropriate for his supervisor to  4._____

    A. reward the employee by giving him an easy assignment next time
    B. avoid praising the employee, since praise without a salary increase is meaningless
    C. praise the employee's work at a later date, provided the employee continues his good work
    D. praise the employee's good work when he has finished the job

5. In order to be granted a paid or unpaid leave of absence on account of illness, an employee must file a written application within _____ after his return to work.  5._____

    A. 2 days  B. 3 days  C. 1 week  D. 2 weeks

6. The transit authority sick leave year ends on  6._____

    A. April 30        B. June 30
    C. September 30    D. December 31

7. Assume that you are the chairman of a meeting attended by ten surface line dispatchers. The BEST course of action to follow initially if you notice that one particular dispatcher is monopolizing the meeting is to

   A. *allow* this dispatcher to talk as much as he wants to since the other men don't wish to speak
   B. *allow* this dispatcher to talk as much as he wants to, otherwise freedom of discussion is curtailed
   C. *interrupt* this dispatcher and warn him not to monopolize the meeting
   D. *interrupt* this dispatcher in a courteous manner and request other members at the meeting to contribute to the discussion

8. When disciplinary charges are specified against a bus operator, the dispatcher normally having the responsibility for giving the operator a copy of the charges and witnessing the receipt of them is _____ dispatcher.

   A. the crew  B. the yard
   C. a senior surface line  D. the general

9. In order for an operator to qualify for 60% sick pay, he must be out sick for AT LEAST _____ consecutive working days.

   A. 7  B. 8  C. 9  D. 10

10. When a supervisor gives orders to a subordinate in connection with a specific task, the amount of explanatory information that the supervisor should give him depends MAINLY on

    A. whether the subordinate appreciates long detailed explanations
    B. the experience of the subordinate and the difficulty of the job
    C. the complexity of the job and how soon it is scheduled to be completed
    D. whether this subordinate has given him trouble in the past

11. Assume that you find that many bus operators by-pass a certain general dispatcher when they are seeking information related to their jobs and, instead, go to others to get the information.
    Of the following reasons, the MOST probable one for the operators by-passing this general dispatcher is that they

    A. do not want to indicate their ignorance to him
    B. have no confidence in his ability to answer their questions
    C. want to make trouble for him
    D. want to obtain information behind his back

12. In case of an accident, an official caution is usually issued to a bus operator when his degree of responsibility is AT LEAST

    A. 25%  B. 50%  C. 75%  D. 90%

13. Assume that you are given an assignment to set up a new safety program for bus operators.
    Of the following, the BEST measure to take FIRST is to

    A. distribute safety literature to the operators
    B. plan your program, seeking suggestions from your subordinates

C. provide detailed lectures to be given by surface line dispatchers
D. indicate to the operators the disciplinary measures that will be taken if they fail to follow approved safety measures

14. A report prepared by general dispatchers on a weekly basis is one that covers   14.____

    A. safety awards        B. vacation pay
    C. salt report          D. restricted duty

15. Disseminating information about surface transportation operations and emergency situations to the various news media is the responsibility of the   15.____

    A. assistant general superintendent, surface transportation
    B. torts department
    C. superintendent - labor relations
    D. public information and community relations department

16. Correspondence having a red tag attached to it means that it   16.____

    A. should be given immediate attention
    B. covers a standard operating procedure
    C. is a confidential document
    D. should be answered within 15 days of receipt

17. The practice of a supervisor in applying fair and firm discipline in all cases of infractions of the rules, including those of a minor nature, should PRIMARILY be considered a(n)   17.____

    A. *desirable* practice, since overlooking minor infractions can lead to a more serious erosion of discipline
    B. *desirable* practice, because violating any rule can cause a hazardous situation
    C. *undesirable* practice, since this will lead to a reduction in organizational efficiency
    D. *undesirable* practice, since discipline for minor violations of the rules is not needed

18. Which of the following statements is TRUE when the probationary period of a newly appointed bus operator is close to expiring and it is found that a decision to terminate or retain him cannot be made with absolute certainty by his supervisor?   18.____

    A. The decision is then made by the superintendent of operations.
    B. The decision is then made by the general dispatcher.
    C. It may be possible to obtain an extension of the probationary period.
    D. The probationary period is automatically extended for a period of 2 months.

19. If, after completing jury duty, an employee receives a jury service check, he must turn in the check to the transit authority within _____ days.   19.____

    A. 5        B. 14        C. 90        D. 120

20. Transit authority bus operators who are legal residents of states other than New York are required to obtain and hold a bus operator's license from   20.____

    A. New York State only
    B. the state of their residence only
    C. both New York State and the state of their residence
    D. the Interstate Commerce Commission

21. When a bus operator observes a taxicab competing with transit authority buses for passengers, the operator is required to submit a written report to

   A. the transit authority police
   B. the nearest road dispatcher
   C. his location chief
   D. the torts department

22. The patrol car log normally contains entries consisting of

   A. bookings
   B. transmitted radio messages
   C. service
   D. split headways

23. At clearing time, the operator's daily trip sheet must be submitted personally to the

   A. yard dispatcher
   B. general dispatcher
   C. location chief
   D. crew dispatcher

24. To compute the last day of work for a bus operator who is scheduled to retire, it is necessary to check the bus operator's record to determine each of the following EXCEPT

   A. the number of AVA days due him
   B. the number of vacation days due him
   C. leaves of absence without pay
   D. his sick leave balance

25. Which of the following statements is TRUE about a bus operator who has lost his badge? He

   A. may not continue to work until he obtains a new one
   B. is permitted to work up to two days without it
   C. must find it before being allowed back to work
   D. will be issued a new one having the same number as the old one

26. If a bus operator marked an *X* in the box for *NO LIGHT* on the surface bus condition report, the trouble would be shown on this report under the category for

   A. Electrical
   B. Miscellaneous
   C. A.C. and Heat
   D. Fare Box

27. On a certain bus route, the one-way running time is 42 minutes and the layover time at each terminal is 6 minutes. If the headway is 8 minutes, then the number of buses required on this route is

   A. 9
   B. 10
   C. 11
   D. 12

Questions 28-40.

DIRECTIONS: Questions 28 through 40 are based on the partly filled-in schedule shown on the following page.

USE THIS SCHEDULE FOR ANSWERING QUESTIONS 28 TO 40

DIVISION: QUEENS
DEPOT: FLUSHING
LINE OR ROUTE: Q-789 JAMES ST.

IN EFFECT: 1-1-04    Week Day    Schedule No. R121

| Run | Report | | | | | | | | | | | | Mileage | Clear |
|---|---|---|---|---|---|---|---|---|---|---|---|---|---|---|
| 1 | AM 349 | P.S. 359 | X 410 | 420 505 | 600 645 | 736 828 | – 850 | R-8 | 940 1008 | 1008 1107 R-3 | – 1133 | R-6 | 39 15 | 1159 |
| 2 | AM 409 | F.O. 419 | X 430 | 440 525 | 616 705 | 752 844 | 945 – | 1008 R-12 | | 1042 1118 R-6 | 1207 1215 | P.I. 1226 | 43 22 | 1236 |
| 3 | AM 429 | P.O. 439 | X 450 | 500 545 | 632 725 | 824 914 | – 940 | R-1 | | 1018 1052 1148 R-5 | – 1214 | R-17 | 39 15 | 1240 |
| 8 | AM 624 | R-1 | 850 – | 924 1020 | – 1046 | R-4 | | 1122 1152 1246 R-7 | | 144 239 336 424 | 457 416 | R-18 | 15 39 | 523 |
| 9 | AM 840 | P.O. 850 | X 901 | 912 1006 | 1103 1158 | 1224 R-16 | | 1255 R-13 | | 224 319 127 | 439 – | R-26 | 28 26 | 505 |
| 25 | PM 357 | R-16 423 | – 455 | – 552 647 | R.O. 736 744 | P.I. 755 | 853 R-31 | | | – 1021 923 1114 | – 1135 | R-30 | 29 22 | 1201 |
| 26 | PM 413 | R-9 439 | – 511 | – 608 703 | 801 854 | – 920 | R-24 | | | 1015 1048 1140 R-28 | 1221 1228 | P.I. 1239 | 37 23 | 1249 |

TIME – HOURS&MINUTES
PAY TIME
TRIPS / SPREAD / TRAVEL / PAY / ALLOWANCE / SWING / NIGHT / OVERTIME / TOTAL PAY TIME

SYMBOLS:
PLAIN TRIPS – Albert St. and Robert St. to John St. and Smith St.
X TRIPS – James St. and Richard St. to Albert St. and Robert St.
RO TRIPS – Albert St. and Robert St. to James St. and Richard St., thence to Depot.
P.O. – Full Out
P.I. – Full In

NOTES:
FROM: Albert St. and Robert St.
Via Albert St., James St., John St. to Smith St.
RETURN: Via John St., James St., Albert St. to Robert St.
RELIEFS MADE AT BRAD ST. AND JOHN ST., VIA ROUTE R-64

28. The boost time for Run No. 25, in minutes, is
    A. 0   B. 2   C. 6   D. 58

29. Of the following runs, the one for which the *night differential* is GREATEST is Run No.
    A. 1   B. 3   C. 9   D. 25

30. The total *travel* allowance for Run No. 2, in minutes, is
    A. 0   B. 16   C. 32   D. 48

31. The operator who has the LEAST *run on* and *run off* trips is the operator on Run No.
    A. 2   B. 3   C. 8   D. 9

32. The TOTAL *travel* allowance for Run No. 8, in minutes, is
    A. 16   B. 32   C. 48   D. 56

33. The *vehicle* time for Run No. 2, in hours and minutes, is
    A. 704   B. 717   C. 733   D. 753

34. Of the following runs, the one which has the MOST *travel* allowance is Run No.
    A. 1   B. 3   C. 9   D. 25

35. Excluding *night differential,* the TOTAL pay for Run No. 3, in hours and minutes, is
    A. 800   B. 811   C. 817   D. 824

36. The TOTAL *pay* for Run No. 26, in hours and minutes, is
    A. 800   B. 826   C. 836   D. 854

37. The TOTAL number of *trips,* including any to and from the depot, for both halves of Run No. 2 is
    A. 10   B. 11   C. 12   D. 13

38. The *spread* for Run No. 8, in hours and minutes, is
    A. 731   B. 829   C. 859   D. 911

39. The overtime *allowance* for Run No. 8, in minutes, is
    A. 0   B. 12   C. 23   D. 35

40. The *night differential* for Run No. 1, in hours and minutes, is
    A. 0   B. 210   C. 349   D. 810

## KEY (CORRECT ANSWERS)

| | | | | | | | |
|---|---|---|---|---|---|---|---|
| 1. | B | 11. | B | 21. | C | 31. | C |
| 2. | C | 12. | C | 22. | B | 32. | B |
| 3. | C | 13. | B | 23. | D | 33. | C |
| 4. | D | 14. | B | 24. | D | 34. | D |
| 5. | B | 15. | D | 25. | A | 35. | B |
| 6. | A | 16. | A | 26. | D | 36. | C |
| 7. | D | 17. | A | 27. | D | 37. | D |
| 8. | D | 18. | C | 28. | A | 38. | C |
| 9. | C | 19. | C | 29. | D | 39. | B |
| 10. | B | 20. | B | 30. | A | 40. | B |

# EXAMINATION SECTION
## TEST 1

DIRECTIONS: Each question or incomplete statement is followed by several suggested answers or completions. Select the one that BEST answers the question or completes the statement. *PRINT THE LETTER OF THE CORRECT ANSWER IN THE SPACE AT THE RIGHT.*

1. In the depot where you are in charge, one of the operators has been the object of numerous practical jokes by unknown co-workers with the result that he has complained to you. You should

    A. inform the operator that this is a personal matter for him to handle
    B. call in each operator and warn them against this practice
    C. refer the operator to the grievance board
    D. try to find the person or persons responsible and prefer charges if advisable

2. In cases involving infraction of rules and regulations by newly appointed surface line operators, the senior surface line dispatcher should

    A. ignore all except serious violations for a short time
    B. treat every operator scrupulously alike
    C. temper discipline with understanding
    D. be particularly strict so that the new operators will respect the rules and regulations

3. You receive evidence that a newly appointed operator is impolite and argumentative with respect to a particular racial group living in the territory of his run. You should

    A. ignore the situation since everyone is prejudiced in one way or another
    B. delegate an operator of the same racial group to reason with the offender
    C. inform the operator that such actions while on duty must cease forthwith or charges will be preferred
    D. transfer the operator to another line in another area

4. A woman passenger reports to the dispatcher at a terminal that she twisted her ankle getting off a bus.
The FIRST action to be taken by the dispatcher is to

    A. arrange for medical attention for the woman
    B. question the woman and examine the ankle to ascertain the seriousness of the alleged injury
    C. inspect the bus to determine whether the condition of the bus was a contributing factor
    D. question the operator in detail about the accident

5. The MAIN advantage of having a detailed schedule of working conditions is that this procedure

    A. standardizes the conditions of employment
    B. removes all inequities
    C. encourages the good worker
    D. is completely automatic in every case

6. Operators should request passengers to step toward the rear of the bus MAINLY to

   A. prevent crowding
   B. be polite to the riding public
   C. increase the amount of revenue collected
   D. accommodate entering passengers

7. A surface line dispatcher desires to check the speed of a certain bus. If he times the bus as travelling 220 feet in 4.9 seconds, then the bus is travelling at, approximately,

   A. 20 m.p.h.
   B. 30 m.p.h.
   C. 36 m.p.h.
   D. 44 m.p.h.

8. The LEAST effective way of reducing overtime would be to

   A. reduce absenteeism
   B. decrease the scheduled time for all runs
   C. keep accurate check of run-off time
   D. increase field supervision

9. Occasionally, 4 bus lines may be substituted for 3 street car lines. The MOST probable reason for the added line is that

   A. the tendency is to restudy and provide better service to the public at the time of the transition
   B. a bus will not accommodate so many people as a street car
   C. street cars can travel much faster than buses
   D. short lines are more efficient for bus service

10. Assume you have been on unfriendly terms with some of the surface line dispatchers in the depot to which you have just been appointed senior surface line dispatcher.
    In this case, the BEST procedure for you to follow would be to

    A. have a confidential talk with them and explain that the past should be forgotten
    B. bear down on them to impress them with the fact that you are the boss
    C. take no action in which they could accuse you of bias
    D. treat them the same as you do the other dispatchers with no mention of the past

11. Because a difficult and complicated grievance peculiar to your depot on which you have been working for the past two weeks had not been decided, the operators suddenly refuse to take out the buses on a certain day.
    As depot supervisor, you should

    A. grant the wishes of the operators at once as the lesser of the two evils
    B. make every effort to convince the men that they are injuring their chances for the most favorable consideration of future grievances
    C. refer the entire matter to the general superintendent's office since it is now out of your hands
    D. tell the men that if they refuse to work charges will be preferred forthwith

12. Assume that you receive a general bulletin order from the assistant general superintendent which you are certain will produce serious consequences in the operation of your depot.
    When you receive this bulletin, you should

A. issue the order as the results will confirm your opinion
B. immediately bring the situation to the attention of the assistant general superintendent through the proper channels
C. issue the order and immediately prepare a report giving your objections
D. issue the order suitably modified for your depot and explain in a report to the assistant general superintendent

13. The situation outlined in the preceding question proves that

    A. it would be better to issue orders separately in each depot
    B. no general order should be issued without consulting with each depot supervisor
    C. the conditions in all depots should be standardized
    D. the depot supervisor should carefully study the effect of each order on his depot

14. If the bus operators on any particular line fail to adhere to the schedule, the responsibility *initially* falls on the

    A. first operator to be late
    B. field inspector
    C. schedule maker
    D. depot supervisor

15. A surface line dispatcher supervising the operation of buses in passenger service normally should devote MOST of his time to

    A. passenger safety
    B. investigating his delays
    C. maintaining regularity of service
    D. answering passenger questions

16. A passenger complaint that a certain bus operator passed a red light is transmitted to you for investigation. The operator admits this act but claims he was justified in doing so. An ACCEPTABLE excuse for this procedure would be that he was

    A. ordered to proceed by a surface line dispatcher
    B. motioned on by a traffic policeman
    C. being followed by a fire truck
    D. late and there was no cross traffic

17. The PRIMARY purpose of the official rules and regulations is to

    A. assist employees in the proper performance of their duties.
    B. provide a basis for disciplinary action
    C. protect the authority against legal actions
    D. relieve supervisory employees of detailed responsibility

18. Operators' watches must be synchronized with the clocks in the dispatcher's office for

    A. absolute accuracy
    B. the operators' convenience
    C. coordination of system operation
    D. saving operators the cost of an expensive watch

19. Passengers are sometimes carried on run-ons and run-offs. In reference to this practice, it is MOST CORRECT to state that

    A. this procedure is confusing to the public
    B. this is a violation of the Police Department traffic regulations
    C. the operator is not likely to object
    D. this is the best procedure to determine whether the line should be extended

20. Assume that you are a senior surface line dispatcher and one of the operators comes to you with a question which should have been settled by the inspector in the field. When asked, the operator says "I discussed it with the inspector and he told me to take it up with you."
    The BEST procedure for you to follow would be to

    A. send the operator back to the inspector for the answer
    B. answer the question and notify the inspector that he should handle such matters himself
    C. call in the inspector together with the operator at their convenience
    D. give the answer to the inspector to relay to the operator

21. Operating employees should not make any statements concerning transit accidents except to employees of the authority in the regular course of business.
    The PROBABLE reason for this rule is to

    A. prevent lawsuits
    B. avoid conflicting testimony
    C. prevent unofficial statements from being accepted as official
    D. conceal facts which may be damaging

22. Preference seniority rosters are posted at various locations throughout the system. The MAIN purpose for this practice is to

    A. minimize absences at picks
    B. decrease the number of picks
    C. prevent errors in records
    D. provide for a more orderly procedure

23. Occasionally, bus operators violate regulations by running "dark" on their run-off to depots. The GREATEST objection to this practice is that the

    A. operator would be more likely to carry unauthorized passengers
    B. accident possibilities are increased
    C. operator will be tempted to exceed speed limits
    D. operator may fall asleep

24. When a bus line replaces a trolley line, the procedure at the depot out of which the bus line will operate is that

    A. a line pick will be required within a 3-day period
    B. a depot pick must be ordered by the assistant general superintendent
    C. regular operators will be sent to the depot until such time as a division pick is held
    D. the street car operators will be transferred to other depots having such service

25. Operators are required to wear prescribed uniforms when on duty. An IMPORTANT reason for this procedure is that such uniforms

   A. tend to improve discipline
   B. inspire respect for superiors
   C. tend to keep the men alert
   D. serve as easy identification

26. A surface line dispatcher should not become over-friendly with the operators under his supervision MAINLY because

   A. it distracts him from his regular duties
   B. it creates an unfavorable impression on other operators
   C. they represent management
   D. he may later be embarrassed if those operators need cautioning

27. If the thickness of material worn from a bus brake lining is, approximately, .20 inch for every 3000 miles of wheel travel, then the number of miles the wheel will have traveled to reduce the thickness from .75 inch to .25 inch is

   A. 3750  B. 6000  C. 7500  D. 11,250

28. A good way for a senior surface line dispatcher to obtain the confidence of his men is to

   A. make no promises unless they can be fulfilled
   B. interpret orders to all employees so that those concerned will receive the greatest possible benefit
   C. be friendly with all subordinates
   D. say as little as possible

29. Operator Smith stopped at a bus stop and dashed into an adjacent restaurant. In his haste he forgot to shut off the motor.
The MOST objectional act committed by this operator was

   A. leaving the bus unattended
   B. going into a restaurant
   C. blocking the bus stop
   D. leaving the motor running

30. A bus operator's uniform should ALWAYS appear neat

   A. to avoid infraction of the rules and regulations
   B. to create a good impression on his superior
   C. since he is in constant contact with the public
   D. since uniform inspections are held frequently

31. A street which accommodated two-way traffic is redesignated as a one-way street. If the immediate result is an increase in accident rate, this is *most likely* due to

   A. increased speed
   B. the accompanying confusion
   C. the increased amount of traffic
   D. new drivers now using this street

32. A bus was standing at its starting terminal and the operator did not open the doors for waiting passengers until his scheduled leaving time.
The MAIN objection to this act was that it

   A. could lead to errors in collecting the fares
   B. delayed the bus unnecessarily
   C. inconvenienced the passengers
   D. might cause an accident to boarding passengers

33. The LEAST likely change in connection with the work of a senior dispatcher in charge of a depot resulting from the transition to a 40-hour week will be

   A. fewer grievances
   B. more work and responsibility
   C. less absenteeism
   D. less lateness

34. The reason for requiring an operator to turn in a remittance slip with his receipts is that it

   A. prevents errors when counting receipts
   B. makes operator dishonesty more difficult
   C. decreases arguments over shortages
   D. simplifies the work for the revenue department

35. Whenever buses are being permanently substituted on an existing trolley line, it is LEAST important to notify

   A. any adjacent subway division since no transfers are permitted
   B. large stores and important businesses in the area since they are not concerned
   C. passengers concerned since there is no change in route
   D. all depots in the bus division since only one depot is concerned

36. Of the following circumstances, the one which indicates MOST emphatically the need for a personal conference between a surface line dispatcher and an operator under his supervision is when the operator

   A. is conscientious in his work but insists on not working overtime
   B. asks many questions about minor details of the general rules and regulations
   C. averages a day off each week because of personal affairs
   D. has had a collision with a fast-moving truck

37. Dispatchers acting as inspectors are required to submit written reports of all unusual occurrences. Of the following, the BEST reason for making the report as soon as possible after the occurrence is that

   A. the report will tend to be more accurate as to facts
   B. the inspector will not be so likely to forget to make the report
   C. there is always a tendency to do a better job under pressure
   D. the report may be too long if made at the inspector's convenience

7 (#1)

38. Operator Canalone, in making out an accident report which involved his bus and a pedestrian, stated in the description, "The bus struck the pedestrian."
This statement on the part of the operator is OBJECTIONABLE because

   A. he should not make any positive statement
   B. it admits that the operator was at fault
   C. it tends to give a conclusion
   D. it is obvious that the pedestrian must have been struck by the bus

38.____

39. Whenever a bus stop is temporarily discontinued, it is MOST necessary to

   A. issue a bulletin to the operators concerned
   B. advise the passengers by notice in the buses concerned
   C. get approval from the general superintendent
   D. adjust the schedule

39.____

40. The proper bus stop should be six inches from the curb. This distance is arrived at by taking into consideration the

   A. convenience of passengers and wear on tires
   B. height of the curb and passenger safety
   C. width of the step and the length of the bus stop area
   D. the various street conditions on all the divisions

40.____

41. Before attempting to settle a group grievance as compared with an individual case, the senior surface line dispatcher should, generally,

   A. take longer to make the decision
   B. check the record for previous complaints of each man in the group
   C. clear his decision with the assistant general superintendent
   D. make a greater effort to give a favorable answer

41.____

42. When bulletin orders are reissued, the purpose is USUALLY to

   A. make sure the order reaches all bulletin boards
   B. supersede prior bulletins
   C. clarify ambiguous rules
   D. keep operators alert to current applications

42.____

43. Several of the provisional surface line operators, who have had considerable service and a good record, have become very careless and unruly, due to the new surface line operators' list which is about to be used. These operators realize that they will be replaced and have decided to "get all they can while they are still able" The BEST procedure to follow would be to

   A. insist that they do the, kind of work they are capable of or resign
   B. report the condition and recommend dismissal of a few of the worst cases
   C. assign the operators to undesirable runs in the hope that they will resign
   D. speed up the appointment of eligibles from the list

43.____

44. A bus depot took in $308,645.00 during a 3-month period. During the following 3-month period, the revenue decreased 17%. The revenue for the second 3-month period, was, most nearly,

   A. $333,890.00    B. $283,400.00    C. $256,175.00    D. $238,655.00

44.____

45. When the route of a line is changed or a bus line is substituted for a trolley line, the number of transfer points is sometimes increased.
    The MOST probable purpose in increasing the number of transfer points is to

    A. increase revenue
    B. improve service
    C. eliminate the need for other changes
    D. decrease the number of buses needed by adjacent lines

46. A decrease in the number of traffic accidents involving buses for a given period of time should be MOST apparent as a result of

    A. increased supervision
    B. safety education of the public
    C. new buses with added safety features
    D. increased care in training the operators

47. Assume that you have been appointed senior surface line dispatcher to a certain depot, but, as a result of sick leave, you did not take over the actual duties until a month later. When you finally take over, there is evidence that the acting depot supervisor, in your absence, has been belittling your abilities and predicting trouble. The acting supervisor is a regular assignee to the depot.
    Your BEST course of action is to

    A. prefer charges against the acting supervisor
    B. keep this employee under the sternest supervision
    C. proceed normally to do the best job possible
    D. compel this employee to make public apology

48. A bus turn-about location at the end of a line is in a good residential neighborhood and constant complaints have been received with respect to noise and fumes during layovers. The MOST effective practical action to be taken would be to

    A. issue a strongly worded bulletin order to the operators
    B. change the location of the turn-about
    C. make a special investigation to determine any possible improvements
    D. explain to the complainants politely and at considerable length why nothing can be done

49. The senior dispatcher of a depot has a surface line dispatcher under his direct supervision whose work requires continuous and direct contact with the operators. The operators complain with respect to the manner and bearing of this dispatcher.
    If the complaint is found to be valid, the senior dispatcher's BEST course of action would be to

    A. prefer charges against the dispatcher since the complaint is valid
    B. inform the operators that the situation was being corrected and have a serious discussion with the dispatcher
    C. advise the dispatcher to ask for a transfer to another depot
    D. support the dispatcher to the operators but warn the dispatcher privately

50. A surface line operator is exceeding a safe speed when he drives faster than road, weather, mechanical or other conditions justify, even though this speed may be lower than the allowable miles per hour.
This means that

   A. the safe speed is primarily a function of the ability of the operator to compensate for abnormal conditions
   B. it is practically impossible for the operator to determine the safe speed under every condition
   C. the safe speed may occur between 0 and 25 miles per hour
   D. there is no absolutely safe speed for operating a bus

51. An operator failing to induce his passengers to move to the rear of the bus will probably be the subject of complaints for

   A. disregarding passenger safety
   B. passing up intending passengers
   C. impoliteness
   D. not adhering to the schedule

52. With respect to the granting of minor privileges to the surface line dispatchers, the senior surface line dispatcher's action should be guided mainly by the thought that

   A. such concessions should be occasionally denied, lest they become too numerous
   B. the granting of such concessions is not one of his perogatives
   C. such concessions should always be based solely on the employee's past record
   D. each case must be considered on its individual merits

53. A surface line dispatcher can be of GREATEST assistance in civil defense while performing his assigned duties by

   A. impressing on the operators the need for alertness
   B. noting the audibility of the sirens
   C. carefully studying all air raid regulations
   D. observing the reactions of pedestrians when test of sirens starts

54. For the most efficient performance of their duties, operators should be thoroughly acquainted with and obey traffic laws to

   A. minimize the number of complaints by the public
   B. avoid receiving summonses
   C. be able to make better time
   D. decrease operational hazards

55. Mileage reports on buses help to determine the

   A. amount the run should pay
   B. time of removal of the bus for overhaul
   C. running time of each bus line
   D. number of buses for schedule requirements

56. The authority has issued bulletins to all its departments requesting cooperation to save water in the growing shortage.
The senior dispatcher in charge of a depot has carried out his responsibility in this matter when he posts the bulletin

   A. without further action because the depot personnel are individually responsible in this case as residents of the city
   B. and makes a personal survey of the depot to locate any possible wastage
   C. and sees to it that the water in each bus is reduced by about 10%
   D. and obtains the signature of each depot employee that he has read the bulletin

57. Where a number of bus lines for different destinations start from the same point, good planning is necessary to avoid passengers embarking on the wrong bus.
The MOST practical and effective procedure is to

   A. have each operator announce the destination of his bus at frequent intervals as passengers embark
   B. make more effective and conspicuous destination signs on the buses
   C. separate the starting points at different locations along the block with appropriate signs
   D. install public address systems at the terminal

58. To properly supervise the operation of buses in passenger service, it is LEAST essential that the surface line dispatcher have

   A. experience on more than one line
   B. close contact with the line's personnel
   C. a location at the most important "time-point"
   D. personal knowledge of traffic conditions on the line

59. Instructions are issued to the inspectors on the surface lines to check seals on coin boxes at every opportunity and to report any irregularities.
The reason for exercising extreme diligence in connection with these seals is that

   A. the seals are expensive
   B. the inspectors are more likely to report such irregularities than the operators
   C. the public comes in contact with coin boxes
   D. it is important to detect tampering at the earliest possible moment

60. Operator Lee was sent into the senior dispatcher's office for being constantly off schedule for the first three days following the effective date of a new schedule. During the interrogation, the senior dispatcher discovered that Brown, who had an excellent record at his former depot, picked the present depot because he had recently moved into this locality. From this interview, it appears that Brown

   A. suddenly lost interest in his work
   B. was trying to obtain some overtime
   C. was unfamiliar with his run
   D. should be given some time off to rest up

## KEY (CORRECT ANSWERS)

| | | | | | | | |
|---|---|---|---|---|---|---|---|
| 1. | D | 16. | B | 31. | B | 46. | D |
| 2. | C | 17. | A | 32. | C | 47. | C |
| 3. | C | 18. | C | 33. | A | 48. | C |
| 4. | A | 19. | A | 34. | D | 49. | B |
| 5. | A | 20. | B | 35. | B | 50. | C |
| 6. | D | 21. | C | 36. | C | 51. | B |
| 7. | B | 22. | D | 37. | A | 52. | D |
| 8. | B | 23. | B | 38. | C | 53. | C |
| 9. | A | 24. | A | 39. | A | 54. | D |
| 10. | D | 25. | D | 40. | A | 55. | B |
| 11. | C | 26. | D | 41. | C | 56. | B |
| 12. | B | 27. | C | 42. | D | 57. | C |
| 13. | D | 28. | A | 43. | B | 58. | A |
| 14. | B | 29. | D | 44. | C | 59. | D |
| 15. | C | 30. | C | 45. | B | 60. | C |

# EXAMINATION SECTION
# TEST 1

DIRECTIONS: Each question or incomplete statement is followed by several suggested answers or completions. Select the one that BEST answers the question or completes the statement. *PRINT THE LETTER OF THE CORRECT ANSWER IN THE SPACE AT THE RIGHT.*

1. Which of the following is the MOST likely action a supervisor should take to help establish an effective working relationship with his departmental superiors?
    A. Delay the implementation of new procedures received from superiors in order to evaluate their appropriateness.
    B. Skip the chain of command whenever he feels that it is to his advantage
    C. Keep supervisors informed of problems in his area and the steps taken to correct them
    D. Don't take up superiors' time by discussing anticipated problems but wait until the difficulties occur

1.____

2. Of the following, the action a supervisor could take which would generally be MOST conducive to the establishment of an effective working relationship with employees includes
    A. maintaining impersonal relationships to prevent development of biased actions
    B. treating all employees equally without adjusting for individual differences
    C. continuous observation of employees on the job with insistence on constant improvement
    D. careful planning and scheduling of work for your employees

2.____

3. Which of the following procedures is the LEAST likely to establish effective working relationships between employees and supervisors?
    A. Encouraging two-way communication with employees
    B. Periodic discussion with employees regarding their job performance
    C. Ignoring employees' gripes concerning job difficulties
    D. Avoiding personal prejudices in dealing with employees

3.____

4. Criticism can be used as a tool to point out the weak areas of a subordinate's work performance.
Of the following, the BEST action for a supervisor to take so that his criticism will be accepted is to
    A. focus his criticism on the act instead of on the person
    B. exaggerate the errors in order to motivate the employee to do better
    C. pass judgment quickly and privately without investigating the circumstances of the error
    D. generalize the criticism and not specifically point out the errors in performance

4.____

5. In trying to improve the motivation of his subordinates, a supervisor can achieve the BEST results by taking action based upon the assumption that most employees
   A. have an inherent dislike of work
   B. wish to be closely directed
   C. are more interested in security than in assuming responsibility
   D. will exercise self-direction without coercion

6. When there are conflicts or tensions between top management and lower-level employees in any department, the supervisor should FIRST attempt to
   A. represent and enforce the management point of view
   B. act as the representative of the workers to get their ideas across to management
   C. serve as a two-way spokesman, trying to interpret each side to the other
   D. remain neutral, but keep informed of changes in the situation

7. A probationary period for new employees is usually provided in many agencies. The MAJOR purpose of such a period is usually to
   A. allow a determination of employee's suitability for the position
   B. obtain evidence as to employee's ability to perform in a higher position
   C. conform to requirements that ethnic hiring goals be met for all positions
   D. train the new employee in the duties of the position

8. An effective program of orientation for new employees usually includes all of the following EXCEPT
   A. having the supervisor introduce the new employee to his job, outlining his responsibilities and how to carry them out
   B. permitting the new worker to tour the facility or department so he can observe all parts of it in action
   C. scheduling meetings for new employees, at which the job requirements are explained to them and they are given personnel manuals
   D. testing the new worker on his skills and sending him to a centralized in-service workshop

9. In-service training is an important responsibility of many supervisors. The MAJOR reason for such training is to
   A. avoid future grievance procedures because employees might say they were not prepared to carry out their jobs
   B. maximize the effectiveness of the department by helping each employee perform at his full potential
   C. satisfy inspection teams from central headquarters of the department
   D. help prevent disagreements with members of the community

10. There are many forms of useful in-service training.
    Of the following, the training method which is NOT an appropriate technique for leadership development is to
    A. provide special workshops or clinics in activity skills
    B. conduct institutes to familiarize new workers with the program of the department and with their roles

C. schedule team meetings for problem-solving, including both supervisors and leaders
D. have the leader rate himself on an evaluation form periodically

11. Of the following techniques of evaluating work training programs, the one that is BEST is to
    A. pass out a carefully designed questionnaire to the trainees at the completion of the program
    B. test the knowledge that trainees have both at the beginning of training and at its completion
    C. interview the trainees at the completion of the program
    D. evaluate performance before and after training for both a control group and an experimental group

11._____

12. Assume that a new supervisor is having difficulty making his instructions to subordinates clearly understood.
    The one of the following which is the FIRST step he should take in dealing with this problem is to
    A. set up a training workshop in communication skills
    B. determine the extent and nature of the communications gap
    C. repeat both verbal and written instructions several times
    D. simplify his written and spoken vocabulary

12._____

13. A director has not properly carried out the orders of his assistant supervisor on several occasions to the point where he has been successively warned, reprimanded, and severely reprimanded.
    When the director once again does not carry out orders, the PROPER action for the assistant supervisor to take is to
    A. bring the director up on charges of failing to perform his duties properly
    B. have a serious discussion with the director, explaining the need for the orders and the necessity for carrying them out
    C. recommend that the director be transferred to another district
    D. severely reprimand the director again, making clear that no further deviation will be countenanced

13._____

14. A supervisor with several subordinates becomes aware that two of these subordinates are neither friendly nor congenial.
    In making assignments, it would be BEST for the supervisor to
    A. disregard the situation
    B. disregard the situation in making a choice of assignment but emphasize the need for teamwork
    C. investigate the situation to find out who is at fault and give that individual the less desirable assignments until such time as he corrects his attitude
    D. place the unfriendly subordinates in positions where they have as little contact with one another as possible

14._____

15. A DESIRABLE characteristic of a good supervisor is that he should     15.____
    A. identify himself with his subordinates rather than with higher management
    B. inform subordinates of forthcoming changes in policies and programs only when they directly affect the subordinates' activities
    C. make advancement of the subordinates contingent on personal loyalty to the supervisor
    D. make promises to subordinates only when sure of the ability to keep them

16. The supervisor who is MOST likely to be successful is the one who     16.____
    A. refrains from exercising the special privileges of his position
    B. maintains a formal attitude toward his subordinates
    C. maintains an informal attitude toward his subordinates
    D. represents the desires of his subordinate to his superiors

17. Application of sound principles of human relations by a supervisor may be expected to _____ the need for formal discipline.     17.____
    A. decrease                B. have no effect on
    C. increase                D. obviate

18. The MOST important generally approved way to maintain or develop high morale in one's subordinates is to     18.____
    A. give warnings and reprimands in a jocular way
    B. excuse from staff conferences those employees who are busy
    C. keep them informed of new developments and policies of higher management
    D. refrain from criticizing their faults directly

19. In training subordinates, an IMPORTANT principle for the supervisor to recognize is that     19.____
    A. a particular method of instruction will be of substantially equal value for all employees in a given title
    B. it is difficult to train people over 50 years of age because they have little capacity for learning
    C. persons undergoing the same course of training will learn at different rates of speed
    D. training can seldom achieve its purpose unless individual instruction is the chief method used

20. Over an extended period of time, a subordinate is MOST likely to become and remain most productive if the supervisor     20.____
    A. accords praise to the subordinate whenever his work is satisfactory, withholding criticism except in the case of very inferior work
    B. avoids both praise and criticism except for outstandingly good or bad work performed by the subordinate
    C. informs the subordinate of his shortcomings, as viewed by management, while according praise only when highly deserved
    D. keeps the subordinate informed of the degree of satisfaction with which his performance of the job is viewed by management.

## KEY (CORRECT ANSWERS)

| | | | |
|---|---|---|---|
| 1. | C | 11. | D |
| 2. | D | 12. | B |
| 3. | C | 13. | A |
| 4. | A | 14. | D |
| 5. | D | 15. | D |
| 6. | C | 16. | D |
| 7. | A | 17. | A |
| 8. | D | 18. | C |
| 9. | B | 19. | C |
| 10. | D | 20. | D |

# TEST 2

DIRECTIONS: Each question or incomplete statement is followed by several suggested answers or completions. Select the one that BEST answers the question or completes the statement. *PRINT THE LETTER OF THE CORRECT ANSWER IN THE SPACE AT THE RIGHT.*

1. A supervisor has just been told by a subordinate, Mr. Jones, that another employee, Mr. Smith, deliberately disobeyed an important rule of the department by taking home some confidential departmental material.
   Of the following courses of action, it would be MOST advisable for the supervisor FIRST to
   A. discuss the matter privately with both Mr. Jones and Mrs. Smith at the same time
   B. call a meeting of the entire staff and discuss the matter generally without mentioning any employee by name
   C. arrange to supervise Mr. Smith's activities more closely
   D. discuss the matter privately with Mr. Smith

1.____

2. The one of the following actions which would be MOST efficient and economical for a supervisor to take to minimize the effect of periodical fluctuations in the workload of his unit is to
   A. increase his permanent staff until it is large enough to handle the work of the busy loads
   B. request the purchase of time- and labor-saving equipment to be used primarily during the busy loads
   C. lower, temporarily, the standards for quality of work performance during peak loads
   D. schedule for the slow periods work that is not essential to perform during the busy periods

2.____

3. Discipline of employees is usually a supervisor's responsibility. There may be several useful forms of disciplinary action.
   Of the following, the form that is LEAST appropriate is the
   A. written reprimand or warning
   B. involuntary transfer to another work setting
   C. demotion or suspension
   D. assignment of added hours of work each week

3.____

4. Of the following, the MOST effective means of dealing with employee disciplinary problems is to
   A. give personality tests to individuals to identify their psychological problems
   B. distribute and discuss a policy manual containing exact rules governing employee behavior
   C. establish a single, clear penalty to be imposed for all wrongdoing irrespective of degree
   D. have supervisors get to know employees well through social mingling

4.____

2 (#2)

5. A recently developed technique for appraising work performance is to have the supervisor record on a continual basis all significant incidents in each subordinate's behavior that indicate unsuccessful action and those that indicate poor behavior.
Of the following, a MAJOR disadvantage of this method of performance appraisal is that it
   A. often leads to overly close supervision
   B. results in competition among those subordinates being evaluated
   C. tends to result in superficial judgments
   D. lacks objectivity for evaluating performance

5.____

6. Assume that you are a supervisor and have observed the performance of an employee during a period of time. You have concluded that his performance needs improvement.
In order to improve his performance, it would, therefore, be BEST for you to
   A. note your findings in the employee's personnel folder so that his behavior is a matter of record
   B. report the findings to the personnel officer so he can take prompt action
   C. schedule a problem-solving conference with the employee
   D. recommend his transfer to simpler duties

6.____

7. When an employee's absences or latenesses seem to be nearing excessiveness, the supervisor should speak with him to find out what the problem is.
Of the following, if such a discussion produces no reasonable explanation, the discussion usually BEST serves to
   A. affirm clearly the supervisor's adherence to proper policy
   B. alert other employees that such behavior is unacceptable
   C. demonstrate that the supervisor truly represents higher management
   D. notify the employee that his behavior is being observed and evaluated

7.____

8. Assume that an employee willfully and recklessly violates an important agency regulation. The nature of the violation is of such magnitude that it demands immediate action, but the facts of the case are not entirely clear. Further, assume that the supervisor is free to make any of the following recommendations.
The MOST appropriate action for the supervisor to take is to recommend that the employee be
   A. discharged              B. suspended
   C. forced to resign        D. transferred

8.____

9. Although employees' titles may be identical, each position in that title may be considerably different.
Of the following, a supervisor should carefully assign each employee to a specific position based PRIMARILY on the employee's
   A. capability     B. experience     C. education     D. seniority

9.____

10. The one of the following situations where it is MOST appropriate to transfer an employee to a similar assignment is one in which the employee
    A. lacks motivation and interest
    B. experiences a personality conflict with his supervisor
    C. is negligent in the performance of his duties
    D. lacks capacity or ability to perform assigned tasks

10.____

11. The one of the following which is LEAST likely to be affected by improvements in the morale of personnel is employee
    A. skill
    B. absenteeism
    C. turnover
    D. job satisfaction

11.____

12. The one of the following situations in which it is LEAST appropriate for a supervisor to delegate authority to subordinates is where the supervisor
    A. lacks confidence in his own abilities to perform certain work
    B. is overburdened and cannot handle all his responsibilities
    C. refers all disciplinary problems to his subordinate
    D. has to deal with an emergency or crisis

12.____

13. Assume that it has come to your attention that two of your subordinates have shouted at each other and have almost engaged in a fist fight. Luckily, they were separated by some of the other employees.
    Of the following, your BEST immediate course of action would generally be to
    A. reprimand the senior of the two subordinates since he should have known better
    B. hear the story from both employees and any witnesses and then take needed disciplinary action
    C. ignore the matter since nobody was physically hurt
    D. immediately suspend and fine both employees pending a departmental hearing

13.____

14. You have been delegating some of your authority to one of your subordinates because of his leadership potential.
    Which of the following actions is LEAST conducive to the growth and development of this individual for a supervisory position?
    A. Use praise only when it will be effective
    B. Give very detailed instructions and supervise the employee closely to be sure that the instructions ae followed precisely
    C. Let the subordinate proceed with his planned course of action even if mistakes, within a permissible range, are made
    D. Intervene on behalf of the subordinate whenever an assignment becomes difficult for him

14.____

15. A rumor has been spreading in your department concerning the possibility of layoffs due to decreased revenues.
    As a supervisor, you should GENERALLY
    A. deny the rumor, whether it is true or false, in order to keep morale from declining

15.____

B. inform the men to the best of your knowledge about this situation and keep them advised of any new information
C. tell the men to forget about the rumor and concentrate on increasing their productivity
D. ignore the rumor since it is not authorized information

16. Within an organization, every supervisor should know to whom he reports and who reports to him.
The one of the following which is achieved by use of such structured relationships is
    A. unity of command
    B. confidentiality
    C. esprit de corps
    D. promotion opportunities

16.____

17. Almost every afternoon, one of your employees comes back from his break ten minutes late without giving you any explanation.
Which of the following actions should you take FIRST in this situation?
    A. Assign the employee to a different type of work and observe whether his behavior changes
    B. Give the employee extra work to do so that he will have to return on time
    C. Ask the employee for an explanation for his lateness
    D. Tell the employee he is jeopardizing the break for everyone

17.____

18. When giving instructions to your employees in a group, which one of the following should you make certain to do?
    A. Speak in a casual, off-hand manner
    B. Assume that your employees fully understand the instructions
    C. Write out your instructions beforehand and read them to the employees
    D. Tell exactly who is to do what

18.____

19. A fist fight develops between two men under your supervision.
The MOST advisable course of action for you to take FIRST is to
    A. call the police
    B. have the other workers pull them apart
    C. order them to stop
    D. step between the two men

19.____

20. You have assigned some difficult and unusual work to one of your most experienced and competent subordinates.
If you notice that he is doing the work incorrectly, you should
    A. assign the work to another employee
    B. reprimand him in private
    C. show him immediately how the work should be done
    D. wait until the job is completed and then correct his errors

20.____

## KEY (CORRECT ANSWERS)

| | | | |
|---|---|---|---|
| 1. | D | 11. | A |
| 2. | D | 12. | C |
| 3. | D | 13. | B |
| 4. | B | 14. | B |
| 5. | A | 15. | B |
| 6. | C | 16. | A |
| 7. | D | 17. | C |
| 8. | B | 18. | D |
| 9. | A | 19. | C |
| 10. | B | 20. | C |

# READING COMPREHENSION
# UNDERSTANDING AND INTERPRETING WRITTEN MATERIAL
# EXAMINATION SECTION
# TEST 1

DIRECTIONS: Each question or incomplete statement is followed by several suggested answers or completions. Select the one that BEST answers the question or completes the statement. *PRINT THE LETTER OF THE CORRECT ANSWER IN THE SPACE AT THE RIGHT.*

Questions 1-6.

DIRECTIONS: Questions 1 through 6, inclusive, are based SOLELY on the information contained in the following paragraphs.

### MODEL XXX BUS AIR SUSPENSION SYSTEM

The bus air suspension system is made up of suspension supports, air bellows, height control valves, radius rods, and shock absorbers. The supports provide the means by which the suspension system is connected to the axles. The system operates automatically and maintains a constant ride height regardless of load or of load distribution.

Vertical loads are supported by eight rubberized nylon air bellows assemblies. Four bellows are used at the front axle, and four double convolution bellows are used at the rear axle. Bellows are installed between beams in the coach body structure and suspension supports attached to axles. The bellows upper bead is clamped between the lower retainer and the piston. When the bellows assembly is installed, the beads form air-tight seals. The rear (double convolution) bellows form seals on the adapter plates which are mounted on the suspension support and upper mounting plate.

The air pressure in the air bellows is varied automatically in proportion to the vehicle load by height control valves. Three height control valves, one at the front axle and two at the rear axle, maintain constant vehicle ride height for all load conditions. The height control valve levers are connected to the axles by links.

The front control valve has a single supply outlet connected to a *tee* in the delivery line to the bellows on both sides.

Radius rods, four at each axle, transmit driving and braking forces from the axles to the coach body. These rods also control the lateral and longitudinal position of each axle under the vehicle. Each end of the radius rod contains a rubber bushing that requires no lubrication. Telescoping type, double-acting shock absorbers are mounted at the ends of each axle. The stabilizer bar, attached in rubber mountings to the body, is linked at both ends to the rear suspension supports.

1. According to the above paragraph, the ride height

   A. varies in proportion to the vehicle load
   B. varies in proportion to bus speed
   C. is constant for all load conditions
   D. varies in proportion to the braking forces

2. The use of double convolution bellows is limited to _____ axle(s).

   A. the right front        B. both front
   C. the right rear         D. both rear

3. The lower retainer is a component which forms a part of the

   A. coach body structure   B. bellows clamp
   C. bellows piston         D. bellows upper bead

4. Air is supplied to the front bellows on both sides through a

   A. tee    B. piston    C. link    D. lever

5. The position of the axles under the vehicle is controlled by the

   A. air bellows            B. height control valves
   C. radius rods            D. shock absorbers

6. The stabilizer bar is

   A. a double-acting type
   B. a telescoping type
   C. installed between beams in the body
   D. linked to the rear suspension supports

Questions 7-12.

DIRECTIONS: Questions 7 through 12, inclusive, are based on the Information for Operators given below. Read this information carefully before answering these items.

### INFORMATION FOR OPERATORS

In spite of caution signs and signal lights, more than 42% of all automobile accidents occur at intersections. In narrow city streets with narrow sidewalks and heavy traffic, you should approach intersections at 15 miles per hour with your foot just touching the brake pedal; in wet weather 10 miles per hour. At rural intersections, be sure you have a clear view of the intersecting road to the right and left at least 300 feet before you reach the intersection, otherwise slow down.

At an intersection, the vehicle on your right has the right-of-way if both of you reach the intersection at the same time. You have the right-of-way over the vehicle at your left under the same condition, but must not insist upon it if there is risk of a collision.

Do not pass another vehicle at an intersection. Stop your vehicle to allow pedestrians to cross in front of you at intersections if they have stepped off the curb. Operators must use extreme caution when approaching or turning at intersections not controlled by a signal light.

7. One of the facts given is that 7.____

   A. nearly all accidents occur at country crossroads
   B. nearly half of all accidents occur at traffic lights in cities
   C. approximately two-fifths of all accidents occur where roads or streets cross one another
   D. 42% of all accidents occur on narrow city streets

8. According to this information, if you are approaching an intersection at which there is no traffic light, and a man has started to cross the street in front of you, you must 8.____

   A. reduce your speed to 15 miles per hour
   B. blow your horn lightly
   C. stop to allow him to cross
   D. place your foot so it just touches the brake pedal

9. At an intersection not protected by a traffic light, you should grant the right-of-way to the vehicle approaching from the 9.____

   A. right if it is 300 feet from the intersection
   B. left if it is 300 feet from the intersection
   C. opposite direction if its right turn indicator is flashing
   D. left or the right if there is danger of a collision

10. In the information, it is clearly stated that an intersection should be approached at 15 miles per hour if you 10.____

    A. are driving on a narrow city street in heavy traffic
    B. do not see a warning sign 300 feet from the intersection
    C. do not intend to pass the vehicle ahead
    D. see a car stopped on the intersecting street waiting to cross

11. The information clearly states that 11.____

    A. most city streets are narrow
    B. all city intersections should be approached at 10 miles per hour
    C. passing another vehicle at an intersection is forbidden
    D. there is a clear view of rural intersections from a distance of 300 feet

12. The type of accident referred to probably does NOT include the striking of a 12.____

    A. pedestrian by a railroad train
    B. pedestrian by a passenger car
    C. bus by a taxicab
    D. bus by a truck

Questions 13-21.

DIRECTIONS: Questions 13 through 21, inclusive, are based on the Bus Operator Instructions given below. Read these instructions carefully before answering these questions.

## BUS OPERATOR INSTRUCTIONS

When running on public streets, operators must have all running lights on during hours of darkness. Practices such as having bus interior lights burning during daylight hours or operating after dark with only half the interior lights burning are forbidden. Tampering with the light circuits and removing fuses therefrom is forbidden. Poor driving practices such as sudden starts and stops, striking curbs, spinning wheels, sliding wheels, riding with hand brake half on, or operating the bus with badly overheated or knocking engine must be avoided. Tires must be frequently inspected to detect improper inflation. When adjusting inside or outside rear view mirrors, the use of force is prohibited, since only mild pressure is required. If adjustment cannot be made by use of mild pressure, report the assembly as defective.

13. Bus operators are forbidden to

    A. inspect tires
    B. remove light fuses
    C. adjust viewing mirrors
    D. stop close to curb

14. The MOST important reason for NOT operating a bus with the engine knocking is to prevent

    A. the noise
    B. loss of power
    C. waste of gas
    D. engine damage

15. A bus operator is required to make a report with respect to

    A. sliding wheels
    B. striking curbs
    C. spinning wheels
    D. stuck mirrors

16. Running lights on a bus operating on city streets would be required before 6 P.M. on every day in the month of

    A. December    B. April    C. June    D. August

17. All interior bus lights should be on when the bus

    A. is garaged for the night
    B. is being repaired
    C. is operating on public streets after dark
    D. fuses are all in place

18. Operating during daylight hours with bus interior lights on is forbidden in order to avoid

    A. a traffic violation
    B. passenger complaints
    C. unsafe bus operation
    D. unnecessary battery drain

19. Riding with the hand brake half on

    A. is a good safety practice
    B. is sometimes permissible
    C. does not cause brake wear
    D. is forbidden

20. The bus operator is required to

    A. repair tires
    B. repair defective mirror assemblies
    C. inspect tires
    D. make sudden starts

21. Making frequent sudden stops would be LEAST likely to cause

    A. improper tire inflation
    B. excessive brake wear
    C. passenger discomfort
    D. rear end collisions

Questions 22-25.

DIRECTIONS: Questions 22 through 25, inclusive, are based on the regulations relating to voting on Primary Day as given below. Read these regulations carefully before answering these questions.

### REGULATIONS RELATING TO VOTING ON PRIMARY DAY

The polls are open from 3:00 to 10:00 P.M. Employees who are on duty Primary Day during the period polls are open, and who would not have two consecutive hours free time to vote, will be granted leave of absence for two hours without loss of pay.

Examples:
1. Employees reporting for work at 3 P.M. to and including 4:59 P.M. will be allowed two hours leave with pay.
2. Employees who report to work at 5 P.M. or thereafter, no time to be allowed.
3. Employees who complete their tour of duty and are cleared on or before 8 P.M., no time to be allowed.

22. A two-hour leave of absence with pay will be granted to employees who are on duty Primary Day if they

    A. have to work two hours while the polls are open
    B. would not have two consecutive hours free time to vote
    C. are working a day tour
    D. are working a night tour

23. An employee working an evening tour will be allowed two hours with pay if he has to report for work at _____ P.M.

    A. 3:00   B. 5:00   C. 7:00   D. 9:00

24. An employee working an afternoon tour will be allowed two hours with pay if he clears at _____ P.M.

    A. 6:00   B. 7:00   C. 8:00   D. 9:00

25. An employee working an afternoon tour will NOT be allowed any time off if he clears at _____ P.M.

    A. 8:00   B. 8:30   C. 9:30   D. 10:00

## KEY (CORRECT ANSWERS)

1. C
2. D
3. B
4. A
5. C

6. D
7. C
8. C
9. D
10. A

11. C
12. A
13. B
14. D
15. D

16. A
17. C
18. D
19. D
20. C

21. A
22. B
23. A
24. D
25. A

# TEST 2

DIRECTIONS: Each question or incomplete statement is followed by several suggested answers or completions. Select the one that BEST answers the question or completes the statement. *PRINT THE LETTER OF THE CORRECT ANSWER IN THE SPACE AT THE RIGHT.*

Questions 1-8.

DIRECTIONS: Questions 1 through 8 are to be answered on the basis of the information contained in the trackmen duties given below. Read these duties carefully before answering these questions.

### TRACKMEN DUTIES

Trackmen will report to and receive orders from assistant foremen of track. Trackmen will install, inspect, repair, replace, and maintain tracks, ties, ballast, track rail fastenings, and track rail electrical insulating joints. Additional duties of trackmen include clearing of tracks in case of accidents, snow removal and tamping of ballast. Further duties of trackmen include such work in train storage yards or on road tracks, within the qualifications of their position, as their superiors may direct.

1. Trackmen receive their orders

    A. only from a foreman of track
    B. from either an assistant foreman or a foreman of track
    C. only from an assistant foreman of track
    D. from any foreman

2. A PROBABLE reason for assigning trackmen to snow removal is because

    A. trackmen cannot do their regular work when it snows
    B. snow removal is heavy work
    C. trackmen can make any necessary repairs at the same time
    D. tracks in yards and on elevated lines must be cleared of snow

3. Inspection of track rails is

    A. performed only by foremen
    B. only done after accidents
    C. the only inspection work performed by a trackman
    D. only one important duty of the trackman

4. A trackman's duties on trackwork do NOT include

    A. replacing track
    B. installing ties
    C. installing insulated joints
    D. repairing station platforms

5. The duties statement shows that trackmen MUST

   A. do any assigned work in connection with track
   B. often act as supervisors
   C. be able to do any work in the subway
   D. do other work when there is no trackwork

6. Tamping is a job USUALLY done in connection with

   A. inspection of insulated joints
   B. ballast work
   C. repair of rail fastenings
   D. snow removal

7. The rail fastenings which trackmen repair are for the

   A. third rail
   B. track rails
   C. turnstile railings
   D. station platform railings

8. The track rail insulated joints are designed to provide _____ insulation.

   A. electrical    B. heat    C. sound    D. vibration

Questions 9-17.

DIRECTIONS: Questions 9 through 17 are to be answered on the basis of the information contained in the Instructions on Trackwork given below. Read these rules carefully before answering these questions.

### INSTRUCTIONS ON TRACKWORK

Tie plates shall be used under rails on all ties except at insulated joints. Bolts through insulating bushings are not to be driven through, but inserted by hand. Guard rails are to be bolted to running rails with standard bolts, using spring washers, head locks, and flat washers. Rail braces shall be spiked with screw spikes. When removing or reinserting screw spikes, care must be taken not to destroy the thread in the wood tie. If a cut spike (nail type) is withdrawn for any reason, the hole is to be filled with a square creosoted plug and the spike re-driven in the same location. Ties are to be pulled by hand. No picks, shovels, or spike mauls are to be used for pulling ties.

9. Ties should be pulled

   A. with spike mauls
   B. with shovels
   C. by hand
   D. with picks

10. Tie plates are used

    A. on all ties
    B. only at insulated joints
    C. except at insulated joints
    D. on alternate ties

11. Rail braces shall have

    A. insulators
    B. bolts
    C. cut spikes
    D. screw spikes

12. Plugs are to be    12.____

    A. square   B. free of creosote
    C. round    D. driven by hand

13. Guard rails are fastened to running rails with    13.____

    A. special bolts   B. standard bolts
    C. insulators      D. plugs

14. Bolts through insulating bushings are to be    14.____

    A. hand inserted   B. non-standard
    C. elliptical      D. driven

15. When cut spikes are withdrawn from a tie, the hole is to be    15.____

    A. insulated   B. rethreaded
    C. left open   D. plugged

16. Head locks and spring washers are used on    16.____

    A. guard rail bolts   B. screw spikes
    C. tie plates         D. cut spikes

17. Screw spike holes in a tie    17.____

    A. may be reused
    B. must be plugged with a round plug
    C. are not to be reused
    D. must always be rethreaded

Questions 18-25.

DIRECTIONS: Questions 18 through 25, inclusive, are to be answered on the basis of the description of the Subway Car Air Compressor System given below. Read this information carefully before answering these questions.

### SUBWAY CAR AIR COMPRESSOR SYSTEM

A two-stage, motor-driven air compressor having a large low pressure cylinder and a smaller high pressure cylinder is used. The low pressure cylinder, fitted with an air intake filter, performs the first stage of compression and discharges through an intercooler into the high pressure cylinder where the second stage of compression is performed. An unloader valve insures that compression does not begin until the motor has reached its full speed. An aftercooler is located between the compressor discharge and a compressor reservoir. An automatic drain valve located on the compressor reservoir automatically discharges precipitated moisture from the reservoir whenever the compressor governor functions to cut in power or shut off power to the compressor motor. The governor operates to stop the compressor when the reservoir air pressure reaches 140 lbs. and to start the compressor when the reservoir air pressure drops to 125 lbs. A safety valve set at 150 lbs. is connected to the compressor reservoir.

18. The number of air cooling devices provided in the compressor system is 18.____
    A. 1    B. 2    C. 3    D. 4

19. When the motor is starting up, it is protected by the 19.____
    A. safety valve    B. governor
    C. drain valve    D. unloader valve

20. The intake filter is MOST likely designed to screen out 20.____
    A. dirt    B. water    C. oil    D. heat

21. The air pressure is LOWEST in the 21.____
    A. small cylinder    B. large cylinder
    C. compressor reservoir    D. aftercooler

22. The automatic drain valve is triggered by the 22.____
    A. governor    B. unloader valve
    C. safety valve    D. intercooler

23. The motor should stop running when the reservoir air pressure reaches _____ lbs. 23.____
    A. 125    B. 130    C. 135    D. 140

24. Water automatically drains from the 24.____
    A. low pressure cylinder    B. high pressure cylinder
    C. air reservoir    D. intercooler

25. Compression begins with the motor 25.____
    A. off    B. at low speed
    C. at intermediate speed    D. at full speed

## KEY (CORRECT ANSWERS)

1. B
2. D
3. D
4. D
5. A

6. B
7. B
8. A
9. C
10. C

11. D
12. A
13. B
14. A
15. D

16. A
17. A
18. B
19. D
20. A

21. B
22. A
23. D
24. C
25. D

# TEST 3

DIRECTIONS: Each question or incomplete statement is followed by several suggested answers or completions. Select the one that BEST answers the question or completes the statement. *PRINT THE LETTER OF THE CORRECT ANSWER IN THE SPACE AT THE RIGHT.*

Questions 1-4.

DIRECTIONS: Questions 1 through 4 are to be answered on the basis of the following information.

## TRESPASSERS ON TRANSIT AUTHORITY SURFACE PROPERTIES

Your attention is again directed to the need for rigid controls to prevent unauthorized persons from entering Transit Authority property.

All strangers or persons who are not recognized as having official business on the property will be questioned by the first member of supervision who encounters them and such persons will be ejected immediately upon failure to present authorization or valid reason for being on the property.

In all cases where trespassers refuse to leave the property, or offer physical resistance to ejection, the Transit Authority police will be promptly notified for assistance and all members of supervision present will assist in the immediate identification and ejection of the trespassers.

Where property protection employees are assigned, they too will be notified.

Immediately following the call for Transit police assistance, notice of the circumstances will be given to Surface Control on Extension B6-504.

All Surface Transportation employees must be advised that entrance and exit from Surface properties must be through authorized locations only, and failure to comply will be considered a flagrant disregard for outstanding regulations.

Finally, a complete written report is to be forwarded to the Assistant General Superintendent, Operations, of all instances dealing with the above.

1. The following are four possible cases that might be correct in which a supervisor may eject a person whom he does not recognize from Transit Authority property: The person
    I. has a legitimate reason for being on Transit Authority property
    II. presents authorization for being on Transit Authority property
    III. has accidently wandered onto Transit Authority property
    IV. has no proof of his identity
   Which of the following choices lists ALL of the above cases that are CORRECT?

   A. I and II
   B. I and III
   C. II and IV
   D. III and IV

1.____

2. If a supervisor is uncertain that a person who he does not know has official business on Transit Authority property, the FIRST action that the supervisor should take is to

   A. eject the person
   B. call the Transit Authority police
   C. call other members of supervision for assistance
   D. question the person

3. When an unauthorized person has been ejected from Transit Authority property, a written report of the incident must be forwarded to

   A. the Superintendent of Operations
   B. Surface Control
   C. the Assistant General Superintendent, Operations
   D. the Location Chief

4. The following are four possible situations that might be CORRECT in which the Transit Authority Police should be notified for assistance:
   I. A trespasser refuses to leave Transit Authority property
   II. A trespasser is encountered on Transit Authority property
   III. A stranger enters Transit Authority property through an unauthorized entrance
   IV. A trespasser physically resists ejection

Questions 5-12.

DIRECTIONS: Questions 5 through 12 are to be answered on the basis of the information contained in the rules for reporting fires given below. Read the rules carefully before answering these questions.

### RULES FOR REPORTING FIRES

If a fire occurs in the subway or in the cars, the person discovering same shall, except in the case of very small fires, go to the nearest telephone and notify the trainmaster. If a fire occurs on a bus, the person discovering same shall, except in the case of very small fires, go to the nearest telephone and notify the Central Dispatch Office. In both cases, the person making the call should give the location of the fire, his name, his badge number, and the department in which employed. In the case of a very small fire, the person discovering same shall use all means in his power to extinguish it promptly using fire extinguishers, sand pails, water buckets, or other equipment readily available. A complete report of the fire, including the location from which the extinguisher or other equipment was taken, should be transmitted promptly to the employee's department head.

5. A fire discovered in the subway should be reported to the

   A. fire department
   B. police department
   C. trainmaster
   D. Central Dispatch Office

6. A fire discovered on a bus should be reported to the

   A. fire department
   B. police department
   C. trainmaster
   D. Central Dispatch Office

7. The employee discovering a fire should report same by use of the NEAREST    7.____

   A. fire alarm box          B. gong
   C. telephone               D. messenger

8. A trackman on duty is LEAST likely to discover a fire    8.____

   A. in the subway           B. on an elevated line
   C. on a bus                D. in a train storage yard

9. The employee discovering a very small fire should    9.____

   A. notify the trainmaster immediately
   B. wait and see if it will spread before reporting it
   C. go for assistance to extinguish it
   D. try to put it out promptly

10. An employee's report on a very small fire would NOT include the    10.____

    A. cost to repair the damage
    B. name of the employee reporting
    C. location of the extinguisher used
    D. date on which the fire occurred

11. The employee's complete report of a fire must identify the extinguisher used MAINLY so that    11.____

    A. it will be refilled or replaced
    B. its effectiveness can be checked
    C. the location of the fire will be recorded
    D. its contents will not be wasted

12. For large fires, the complete report required in the last sentence of the above rules is a written report because    12.____

    A. a written report is most accurate
    B. the fire may involve a criminal offense
    C. the original report was made orally
    D. it provides a permanent record

Questions 13-22.

DIRECTIONS:  Questions 13 through 22, inclusive, are to be answered on the basis ONLY of the Description of Porter's Equipment given below. Read this description carefully before answering these questions.

### DESCRIPTION OF PORTER'S EQUIPMENT

The Tampico Brush has white hard bristles and is used to apply soap solution when cleaning columns and tile. The Palmyra Brush has very hard red bristles and is used to scrub gutters, booth floors, and urinal stands. The Milwaukee Push Broom is approximately 3 feet in length, with black semi-hard bristles and is used for sweeping floors. The Rinsing Brush has very soft bristles and is used to wash away all soap solution after surfaces have been scrubbed. The Fibre Broom has reddish-brown stiff fibres, and is used to sweep stairways. Utility Boxes, containing compartments for sawdust, sand, and salt, are located at the ends of station platforms.

13. Stairway steps are cleaned with the 13.\_\_\_\_

    A. Push Broom     B. Tampico Brush
    C. Palmyra Brush     D. Fibre Broom

14. The Push Broom has a length of APPROXIMATELY _____ inches. 14.\_\_\_\_

    A. 48     B. 36     C. 20     D. 18

15. Soap solution is applied to tile with a _____ brush. 15.\_\_\_\_

    A. Palmyra     B. soft-bristle
    C. red-bristle     D. Tampico

16. The brush with very soft bristles is used for 16.\_\_\_\_

    A. rinsing     B. sweeping     C. scrubbing     D. dusting

17. The material which is LEAST likely to be stored in a Utility Box is 17.\_\_\_\_

    A. sand     B. salt     C. sawdust     D. soap

18. Columns are cleaned with the 18.\_\_\_\_

    A. Fibre Broom     B. Push Broom
    C. Tampico Brush     D. Palmyra Brush

19. The Fibre Broom has fibres whose color is 19.\_\_\_\_

    A. pure white     B. solid red
    C. jet black     D. reddish-brown

20. Sand is stored at the 20.\_\_\_\_

    A. booths     B. stairways
    C. exit gates     D. platform ends

21. The MINIMUM number of compartments in the Utility Boxes must be 21.\_\_\_\_

    A. 4     B. 3     C. 2     D. 1

22. Urinal stands are scrubbed with a 22.\_\_\_\_

    A. Tampico Brush     B. Push Broom
    C. Rinsing Brush     D. Palmyra Brush

Questions 23-25.

DIRECTIONS: Questions 23 through 25 are to be answered SOLELY on the basis of the following Directive. Read this Directive carefully before answering the questions.

## DIRECTIVE

When work trains having miscellaneous equipment (flat cars, crane cars, etc.) are in transit, the following flagging and safety instructions must be adhered to:

1. When flat cars are at the forward end of a train, the Flagman will station himself on the leading car. The Flagman will keep in constant communication with the Motorman through the use of sound-powered telephones. If sound-powered telephones become defective and alternate means of communications are needed, the Command Center must be called for instructions. Positive communications must be maintained while the train is in motion. Any loss of communication will be a signal for the Motorman to *Stop and Investigate*.

2. When flat cars are trailing, the Flagman will station himself on the rear of the last motor car in a position to view the trailing cars. Flagmen must observe that tail lights are illuminated at all times.

3. At all times when these trains are stopped for any reason, Motorman must sound two blasts of the whistle or horn before proceeding.

4. Safety demands that Motormen and Flagmen investigate all causes of a train going into emergency; particularly when an employee is known to be riding a flat car.

5. Under no circumstances will an employee walk across a flat car while a train is in motion.

23. When flat cars are at the forward end of a work train, the Flagman will station himself _____ car.

    A. at the rear of the last motor
    B. on the trailing flat
    C. on the leading flat
    D. at the front of the first motor

24. When a train with flat cars has stopped and the Motorman wishes to proceed again, he MUST

    A. call the Command Center
    B. shout instructions to the Flagman
    C. check that the Flagman is using the correct signals
    D. sound two blasts of the whistle or horn

25. When there is a loss of positive communication between the Motorman and the Flagman while the train is in motion, the Motorman should

    A. tell the Flagman to use his flashlight for flagging
    B. stop the train and investigate the situation
    C. tell the Flagman to use hand signals for flagging
    D. put the train into emergency

## KEY (CORRECT ANSWERS)

1. D
2. D
3. C
4. B
5. C

6. D
7. C
8. C
9. D
10. A

11. A
12. D
13. D
14. B
15. D

16. A
17. D
18. C
19. D
20. D

21. B
22. D
23. C
24. D
25. B

# ARITHMETICAL REASONING
# EXAMINATION SECTION
# TEST 1

DIRECTIONS: Each question or incomplete statement is followed by several suggested answers or completions. Select the one that BEST answers the question or completes the Statement. *PRINT THE LETTER OF THE CORRECT ANSWER IN THE SPACE AT THE RIGHT.*

1. The weekly pay for 8 hours a day, 5 days a week, at $16.8750 an hour can be calculated as

    A. 5 x 8 x 16.8570  
    B. 8 + 5 x 16.8750  
    C. 8 x 5 x 16.8750  
    D. 8 + 5 x 16.8570

    1.____

2. A bus operator starts out with $10.00 in change, and his fare box indicates he collects $85.50 in passenger fares. On counting his money, he finds he has 75 one dollar bills, 10 fifty cent pieces, 22 quarters, and 70 dimes.
    To have the CORRECT amount, the number of nickels he should have is

    A. 45   B. 50   C. 55   D. 60

    2.____

3. The register on the fare box of a certain bus has 5 dials and shows the total number of cents collected. When a particular bus operator starts his tour of duty, the register reading is 08980, and at the conclusion of his tour of duty the reading is 14540.
    The TOTAL number of 20-cent fares collected during this operator's tour was

    A. 278   B. 598   C. 783   D. 969

    3.____

4. A particular bus has 12 cross seats holding two passengers each, plus rear and longitudinal seats holding a total of 14 additional passengers.
    If the number of standees permitted on a bus is one-half the number of seated passengers, the TOTAL passenger capacity of this bus is

    A. 26   B. 38   C. 39   D. 57

    4.____

5. A crosstown bus operates between two terminals 22 blocks apart and makes 18 stops. It takes half a minute to travel each block and a quarter of a minute at each stop, and 5 minutes are lost at traffic lights.
    The TOTAL time required to go from one terminal to the other is _____ minutes.

    A. 15 1/2   B. 17 1/2   C. 20 1/2   D. 22 1/2

    5.____

6. The TOTAL value of an operator's change fund consisting of 7 half-dollars, 19 quarters, 169 dimes, and 105 nickels is

    A. $28.40   B. $29.40   C. $30.40   D. $31.40

    6.____

7. If it takes a bus 30 seconds to pass two checkpoints that are 500 feet apart, then the speed of the bus is APPROXIMATELY _____ m.p.h.

    A. 10.1   B. 11.4   C. 12.7   D. 14.2

    7.____

2 (#1)

8. If the length of a particular bus route is 8.6 miles and the average speed of a bus on this route is 7.5 miles per hour, then the ONE-WAY running time for a bus is _____ minutes.   8.___

   A. 52.3    B. 64.5    C. 68.8    D. 75.6

9. If your watch gains 20 minutes per day and you set it to the correct time at 7:00 A.M., the correct time, to the NEAREST minute, when the watch indicates 1:00 P.M. is   9.___

   A. 12:50    B. 12:56    C. 1:05    D. 1:10

10. A particular bus seats 34 passengers and stands half that number.
    The TOTAL passenger capacity of the bus is   10.___

    A. 41    B. 51    C. 61    D. 68

11. The fare register box on a bus shows the total number of cents collected. At the beginning of a run, the register reading of a certain box was 15750 and at the end of the run the reading was 17150.
    The TOTAL number of $1.00 fares collected during the run was   11.___

    A. 16    B. 17    C. 14    D. 19

12. Manuals on driving stress the importance of allowing ample braking distance to the car ahead, the most common rule of thumb being to allow a car length for each ten miles per hour of speed.
    If the overall length of a car is 210 inches, the proper braking distance to allow at a speed of 40 miles per hour is NEAREST to _____ feet.   12.___

    A. 700    B. 500    C. 70    D. 50

13. A bus requires 40 minutes to go from one terminal to another and stops for 10 minutes at each terminal. The MAXIMUM number of one-way trips that the bus can complete in 6 hours is   13.___

    A. 6    B. 7    C. 8    D. 9

Questions 14-21.

DIRECTIONS: Questions 14 through 21 in Column I are questions of simple arithmetic, each of which has one of the answers listed in Column II. For each item in Column I, select the CORRECT answer from Column II.

| COLUMN I | COLUMN II | |
|---|---|---|
| 14. 229 times 9 | A. 1,383 | 14.___ |
| 15. 11,064 divided by 8 | B. 1,752 | 15.___ |
| 16. 1,384 plus 368 | C. 2,061 | 16.___ |
| 17. 3,021 minus 447 minus 386 | D. 2,682 | 17.___ |
| 18. 149 times 3 times 6 | E. 2,188 | 18.___ |
| 19. 727 plus 17 plus 639 | | 19.___ |

20. 2,881 minus 693                                                                   20.____

21. 43,281 divided by 3 divided by 7                                                  21.____

Questions 22-25.

DIRECTIONS:  Questions 22 through 25 in Column I are questions of simple arithmetic, each of which has one of the answers listed in Column II. For each item in Column I, select the CORRECT answer from Column II.

| COLUMN I | COLUMN II | |
|---|---|---|
| 22. 198 times 3 times 4 | A. 1,267 | 22.____ |
| 23. 837 plus 18 plus 412 | B. 2,376 | 23.____ |
| 24. 8,869 divided by 7 | C. 1,944 | 24.____ |
| 25. 2,693 minus 509 | D. 1,867 | 25.____ |
|  | E. 2,184 |  |
|  | F. 2,076 |  |

---

# KEY (CORRECT ANSWERS)

1. C                    11. C
2. D                    12. C
3. A                    13. B
4. D                    14. C
5. C                    15. A

6. C                    16. B
7. B                    17. E
8. C                    18. D
9. B                    19. A
10. B                   20. E

21. C
22. B
23. A
24. A
25. E

---

## SOLUTIONS TO PROBLEMS

1. Weekly pay = 5 x 8 x 16.8750
2. $10.00 + $85.50 - ($75+$5+5.50+$7) = $3 = 60 nickels
3. 14,540 - 08980 = 05560, and 5560 ÷ 20 = 278
4. Number of people sitting = (12)(2) + 14 = 38. Number of people on bus = 38 + (1/2)(38) = 57
5. Total time = (22)(1/2) + (18)(1/4) + 5 = 20.5 minutes
6. (7)(.50) + (19)(.25) + (169)(.10) + (105)(.05) = $30.40
7. 500 ft in 30 sec = 16 2/3 ft per sec. Since 60 mph = 88 ft per sec, the bus' speed = (60)(16 2/3/88) 11.4 mph
8. Let x = number of minutes. Then, 7.5/60 = 8.6/x. Solving, x = 68.8
9. If the watch gains 20 mins. in 24 hrs., it gains 5/6 min. or 50 seconds in 1 hour. In 6 hours, from 7:00 AM to 1:00 PM, it gains 5 mins: (6 x 5/6). When the watch indicates 1:00 PM, the correct time is 12:55 PM.
10. Passenger capacity = 34 + (1/2)(34) = 51
11. 17150 - 15750 = 1400, so 1400 cents = 14 $1 fares
12. (210 in.)(40/10) = 840 in. = 70 ft.
13. 6 hrs. ÷ 5/6 hr. = 7.2, so 7 trips would be the maximum number.
14. (229)(9) = 2061
15. 11,064 ÷ 8 = 1383
16. 1384 + 368 = 1752
17. 3021 - 447 - 386 = 2188
18. (149)(3)(6) = 2682
19. 727 + 17 + 639 = 1383
20. 2881 - 693 = 2188
21. 43,281 ÷ 3 ÷ 7 = 2061
22. (198)(3)(4) = 2376
23. 837 + 18 + 412 = 1267
24. 8869 ÷ 7 = 1267
25. 2693 - 509 = 2184

# TEST 2

DIRECTIONS: Each question or incomplete statement is followed by several suggested answers or completions. Select the one that BEST answers the question or completes the statement. *PRINT THE LETTER OF THE CORRECT ANSWER IN THE SPACE AT THE RIGHT.*

1. A bus depot took in $308,645.00 during a 3-month period. During the following 3-month period, the revenue decreased 17%.
   The revenue for the second 3-month period was MOST NEARLY

   A. $333,890.00  B. $283,400.00
   C. $256,175.00  D. $238,655.00

   1.____

2. A surface line dispatcher desires to check the speed of a certain bus.
   If he times the bus as traveling 220 feet in 4.9 seconds, then the bus is traveling at APPROXIMATELY _____ m.p.h.

   A. 20  B. 30  C. 36  D. 44

   2.____

3. If the thickness of material worn from a bus brake lining is approximately .20 inch for every 3,000 miles of wheel travel, then the number of miles the wheel will have traveled to reduce the thickness from .75 inch to .25 inch is

   A. 3,750  B. 6,000  C. 7,500  D. 11,250

   3.____

4. A dispatcher desires to check the speed of a certain 40-foot bus.
   If he times the bus as passing him in 1.5 seconds, then the bus is traveling at APPROXIMATELY _____ m.p.h.

   A. 15  B. 18  C. 22  D. 27

   4.____

5. The number of feet required to bring a bus traveling at 30 m.p.h. to a stop at a braking rate of 3 miles per hour per second is NEAREST to _____ feet.

   A. 180  B. 200  C. 220  D. 240

   5.____

6. A bus leaves one time point at 10:35 and arrives at the next time point at 11:00.
   If the distance between the time points is 3 miles, the average speed of the bus, in m.p.h., was MOST NEARLY

   A. 6  B. 6 1/2  C. 7  D. 7 1/2

   6.____

7. Eighty percent of the 300 operators in your depot are married, and 50% of all operators are under 35 years of age.
   The MINIMUM number of married operators in this lower age group is

   A. 60  B. 90  C. 150  D. 240

   7.____

8. A bus maintained a speed of 5 m.p.h. for one-third of its route, 10 m.p.h. for the second third, and 15 m.p.h. for the final third.
   The AVERAGE speed for the entire route was CLOSEST to _____ m.p.h.

   A. 8  B. 9  C. 10  D. 11

   8.____

125

9. During the month of August, approximately 900,000 more passengers used the surface lines than during the same month the year before. This was an increase of about 3%. The total number of passengers who used this surface transportation system during August was NEAREST to

   A. 3,000,000
   B. 3,900,000
   C. 29,000,000
   D. 31,000,000

10. Assume that there are 300 bus operators at terminal A. Terminal B has 85% as many bus operators as terminal A, and terminal C has 90% as many bus operators as terminal B. The number of operators assigned to terminal C is NEAREST to

    A. 230   B. 245   C. 255   D. 270

11. A bus leaves the terminal on time at 11:48 A.M. and after one roundtrip returns 11 minutes late at 1:06 P.M. It leaves again on time at 1:12 P.M.
    If the scheduled recovery time at both ends of the line is the same, the scheduled terminal-to-terminal running time, in minutes, is

    A. 25   B. 33   C. 42   D. 50

12. A bus line had a schedule headway of 6 minutes. Run #7 left the near terminal at 10:45 A.M. and shortly thereafter had to be taken out of service on account of engine trouble. Its passengers were picked up by its follower, run #8. The delay caused run #8 to arrive at the far terminal 6 minutes late.
    If the time of arrival of run #8 was 11:53 A.M., then the scheduled running time for the trip was _____ minutes.

    A. 44   B. 56   C. 68   D. 96

13. If a fuel storage tank contains 11,200 gallons of fuel when it is 85% full, its MAXIMUM capacity, in gallons, is CLOSEST to

    A. 9,589   B. 13,175   C. 13,274   D. 14,107

14. Assume that a total of 345 people are employed at a certain location.
    If 2/5 of these people report to work at 7:00 A.M. and another 1/5 at 8:00 A.M., then the number of people that have NOT yet reported to work is

    A. 73   B. 138   C. 154   D. 199

15. Assume that a bus consumes an average of 8 gallons of fuel per hour and that each gallon of fuel weighs 7 1/4 pounds.
    In a 6 hour period, the amount of fuel used, in pounds, is

    A. 108   B. 232   C. 348   D. 399

16. The opening Metrocard reading on a daily register is 1,152, and the last Metrocard closing reading is 1,463. The opening cash reading is 12,015, and the last cash closing reading is 24,345. (Reading increases by 30 for each fare.) The total number of revenue-paying passengers that this bus carried on this day is CLOSEST to

    A. 722   B. 1,112   C. 1,463   D. 12,330

17. If it takes a bus 30 seconds to pass two checkpoints that are 500 feet apart, then the speed of the bus is APPROXIMATELY _____ m.p.h.

    A. 10.1     B. 11.4     C. 12.7     D. 14.2

18. If the length of a particular bus route is 8.6 miles and the average speed of a bus on this route is 7.5 miles per hour, then the one-way running time for a bus is _____ minutes.

    A. 52.3     B. 64.5     C. 68.8     D. 75.6

19. A certain bus route is five miles long. The schedule speed for half of the route is 6 m.p.h., and for the other half of the route it is 15 m.p.h.
    The AVERAGE schedule speed for the entire route

    A. is between 6 m.p.h. and 10.5 m.p.h.
    B. is exactly 10.5 m.p.h.
    C. is between 10.5 m.p.h. and 15 m.p.h.
    D. cannot be calculated without knowing running time for each half of the route

20. A regular tour of duty for an operator requires him to report at 5:50 A.M., leave on his first run at 6:05 A.M., swing from 10:30 A.M. to 2:00 P.M., complete his last.
    run at 5:10 P.M., and clear/at 5:20 P.M. (Notpaid ..for swing time.) The normal pay for this tour is at the operator's regular rate for _____ hours, _____ minutes.

    A. 9; 30     B. 9; 45     C. 10; 15     D. 11; 30

21. An employee who has a wristwatch which gains 30 minutes per day sets it to the correct time at 6:00 A.M.
    When the watch indicates 12:00 Noon, the CORRECT time, to the nearest minute, is

    A. 11:46     B. 11:53     C. 12:07     D. 12:14

22. The one-way running time on a bus route is 1 hour and 6 minutes, and the average speed of a bus on this route is 14 m. p.h.
    What is the length, in miles, of this route?

    A. 13.5     B. 14.0     C. 14.4     D. 15.4

23. A bus consumes 45 gallons of fuel after having traveled a distance of 328 miles.
    The number of miles per gallon of fuel that this bus gets, based on this information, is CLOSEST to

    A. 6.8     B. 7.3     C. 7.8     D. 8.3

24. A bus operator with a weekday run whose hourly rate of pay is $12.60 normally reports for work at 7:30 A.M. and clears at 3:00 P.M.(On report days he works until 4 P.M.) What is his gross pay for a day on which he is required to write an accident report at the end of his run?

    A. $107.10     B. $108.90     C. $113.40     D. $115.60

25. A passenger count was made at a certain terminal between 8 A.M. and 9 A.M., and it was noted that eight buses were loaded with the following number of passengers: 34, 52, 29, 63, 19, 17, 56, and 42, respectively.
The TOTAL number of passengers boarding these eight buses was

   A. 302       B. 312       C. 313       D. 412

25.\_\_\_

## KEY (CORRECT ANSWERS)

1. C
2. B
3. C
4. B
5. C

6. C
7. B
8. A
9. D
10. C

11. A
12. B
13. B
14. B
15. C

16. A
17. B
18. C
19. A
20. B

21. B
22. D
23. B
24. A
25. B

# SOLUTIONS TO PROBLEMS

1. ($308,645)(.83) ≈ $256,175

2. 220 ft. in 4.9 sec ≈ 45 ft. per sec. Since 60 mph means 88 ft.per sec., the bus is moving at (60)(45/88) ≈ 30 mph

3. .75 - .25 = .50. Then, (3000) (.50/.20) = 7500 miles

4. 40 ft. in 1.5 sec. = 26 2/6 ft. per sec. Thus, the bus is moving at (60)(26 2/3/88) ≈ 18 mph

5. Initial speed is 30 mph = 44 ft. per sec. Final speed (when fully stopped) is 0 ft. per sec. Average speed = 22 ft. per sec. Distance = (average speed)(time) = (22)(10 sec.) = 220 ft.

6. 3 miles in 25 min. means (3)(60/25) = 7.2 ≈ 7 mph

7. Let x = minimum number of married operators under 35 years old. Then, 240-x = number of married operators over 35 years old, and 150-x = number of unmarried operators under 35 years old. Since there are probably operators who are neither married nor under 35 years old, (240-x) + (x) + (150-x) ≤ 300. Solving, x ≥ 90.

8. 5 mph= 1/3; 10 mph= 1/3; 15 mph= 1/3. 5 + 10 + 15= 30. 30 divided by 3= 10 mph average speed.

9. 900,000 ÷ .03 = 30,000,000. Then, 30,000,000 + 900,000 = 30,900,000 ≈ 31,000,000 passengers in August.

10. Terminal B has (300X.85) = 255 operators, so terminal C has (255)(.90) ≈ 230 operators.

11. The scheduled running time for a roundtrip from 11:48 AM to 12:55 PM is 67 minutes. Since the recovery time is 17 minutes (12:55 PM - 1:12 PM), and recovery time must only be deducted once from the running time for a roundtrip, the scheduled running time from terminal to terminal is $\frac{67-17}{2} = \frac{50}{2} = 25$

12. From 10:45 AM to 11:53 AM is 68 minutes. Then, 68 - 6 - 6 = 56 minutes for the scheduled running time.

13. 11,200 ÷ .85 ≈ 13,176, closest to 13,175 gallons

14. (1 - 2/5 - 1/5)(345) = 138 people

15. (6)(8)(7 1/4) = 348 pounds of fuel

16. Number of people paying by Metrocard = 1463 - 1152 = 311 Number of people paying by cash = (24,345-12,015) ÷ 30 = 411 Total of individuals paying revenue = 722

17. 500 ft. in 30 sec. means 16 2/3 ft. per sec. Then, the speed of the bus = (60)(16 2/3 ÷ 88) ≈ 11.4 mph

18. 8.6 ÷ 7.5 = 1.14$\overline{6}$ hrs. = 68.8 min.

19. Times for each half are $\frac{2.5}{6}$ = .41$\overline{6}$ hrs. and $\frac{2.5}{15}$ = .1$\overline{6}$ min. Average speed = 5 ÷ (.41$\overline{6}$ + .1$\overline{6}$) ≈ 8.6 mph; thus, it is between 6 mph and 10.5 mph.

20. His tour extends from 5:50 AM to 5:20 PM, for a total period of 11 1/2 hours, less swing time from 10:30 AM to 2:00 PM, which is 3 1/2 hours. 11 1/2 - 3 1/2 = 8 hours

21. 30 min/1440 min = $.0208\overline{3}$ gain. Thus, 6 hrs. on the watch indicates $6 \div 1.0208\overline{3} \approx 5.88$ hrs. hrs. $\approx$ 5 hrs. 53 min. in actual time. The actual time is 11:53 AM.

22. Let x = miles on this route. Then, $\dfrac{14}{x} = \dfrac{1\text{hr.}}{1.10\text{hrs.}}$ Solving, x = 15.4

23. $328 \div 45 \approx 7.3$ miles per gallon

24. 7:30 AM to 4:00 PM = 8 1/2 hrs. Then, ($12.60)(8.5) = $107.10

25. 34 + 52 + 29 + 63 + 19 + 17 + 56 + 42 = 312 passengers

# TEST 3

DIRECTIONS: Each question or incomplete statement is followed by several suggested answers or completions. Select the one that BEST answers the question or completes the statement. *PRINT THE LETTER OF THE CORRECT ANSWER IN THE SPACE AT THE RIGHT.*

1. The total automobile traffic of a bridge increased from 33,000 to 37,000. This represents an increase of APPROXIMATELY

    A. 8%  B. 12%  C. 16%  D. 20%

    1._____

2. Eighty percent of the vessels passing under a certain bridge are tugboats. If 105 vessels pass under this bridge daily, the number of tugboats passing under the bridge daily is

    A. 80  B. 84  C. 88  D. 92

    2._____

3. A certain shelf can safely hold 140 pounds. On the shelf is a 45 pound carton of nuts and bolts, a 52 pound carton of assorted hardware, and two containers of lead paint weighing 27 lbs. each.
The shelf

    A. is overloaded by 16 lbs.
    B. can safely hold an additional 16 lbs.
    C. is overloaded by 11 lbs.
    D. can safely hold an additional 11 lbs.

    3._____

4. Of the following decimals, the one which has the same value as 3/8 is

    A. 0.125  B. 0.266  C. 0.333  D. 0.375

    4._____

5. If an iron bar 6'6 1/8" long is cut in half, the length of each piece will then be MOST NEARLY

    A. 3'3 1/16"   B. 3'3 1/8"
    C. 3'6 1/8"    D. 3'6 1/4"

    5._____

6. The amount of liquid that can be stored in 72 one-quart cans is _____ gallons.

    A. 9  B. 18  C. 24  D. 36

    6._____

7. Suppose that an officer carried two packages, one weighing 73 pounds and the other weighing 41 pounds 3 ounces.
The DIFFERENCE between the weights of the two packages was _____ pounds _____ ounces.

    A. 31; 5  B. 31; 13  C. 32; 6  D. 32; 12

    7._____

8. Suppose that the toll money collected at a bridge during March of last year was $153,696.
If the toll money collected at this bridge in April was 3% higher than in March, then the April total was MOST NEARLY

    A. $149,085  B. $158,307  C. $167,431  D. $200,075

    8._____

131

9. Suppose that 10% more vehicles crossed a certain bridge on Friday than on the previous day.
   If 18,100 cars, 1,290 trucks, and 130 buses used the bridge on Thursday, how many cars, trucks, and buses crossed the bridge on Friday?
   A. 17,568   B. 18,144   C. 19,520   D. 21,472

10. The maximum height allowed for vehicles using a particular bridge under normal conditions is 13 feet 6 inches.
    If a vehicle is 15 feet 5 inches tall, by exactly what amount does the vehicle EXCEED the maximum height limit for this bridge?
    _____ foot(feet) _____ inch(es).
    A. 1; 9   B. 1; 11   C. 2; 1   D. 2; 3

11. The number of cars, trucks, and buses using two different toll lanes on a certain day was as follows:

    |        | Lane 1 | Lane 2 |
    |--------|--------|--------|
    | Cars   | 994    | 1,086  |
    | Trucks | 113    | 51     |
    | Buses  | 31     | 16     |

    A comparison of these two lanes would show that the TOTAL number of cars, trucks, and buses using Lane 1 on that day was _____ than the total at Lane 2.
    A. 15 fewer   B. 25 fewer   C. 15 more   D. 25 more

12. A certain officer was assigned to collect tolls for two hours. The officer was given $80 in various bills and $150 in quarters so that he could make change. He placed this money in a drawer in the toll booth. At the end of the two hours of toll collecting, the officer had a total of $1,375.75 in the drawer.
    The percent of this total which represents the tolls collected is MOST NEARLY
    A. 15%   B. 63%   C. 78%   D. 83%

13. The number of vehicles using a particular lane each hour during a 6-hour period varied as follows: 134, 210, 213, 234, 111, and 118.
    The AVERAGE number of vehicles per hour using the toll lane during this period was
    A. 150   B. 160   C. 170   D. 180

14. Assume that you have been assigned to a shift which begins at 2:00 P.M., and you want to arrive 10 minutes before the shift begins. If you average 28 miles per hour while driving to work and must travel 21 miles, at exactly what time should you start driving to work?
    A. 12:30 P.M.   B. 12:40 P.M.
    C. 1:05 P.M.    D. 1:15 P.M.

15. A rectangular storage room is 15 ft. by 16 ft., and the ceiling height is 10 feet.
    The volume of this room, in cubic feet, is
    A. 2,200   B. 2,300   C. 2,400   D. 2,500

16. One-quarter of the 168 light bulbs on a certain bridge are replaced during the year. If these bulbs cost the city 21 cents each, the yearly cost of replacing the bulbs is

    A. $8.40   B. $8.82   C. $8.86   D. $8.92

17. If 14,229 is divided by 17, the answer is

    A. 737   B. 747   C. 837   D. 847

18. A worker receives $171.50 per day.
    In 15 working days, his TOTAL earnings should be

    A. $2,560.50   B. $2,562.50
    C. $2,570.50   D. $2,572.50

19. If an Assistant Bridge Operator earns $24,500 in the first six months of a year and receives a 10% raise in salary for the next six months of the same year, his total earnings for the year will be

    A. $50,900   B. $51,450   C. $52,750   D. $53,950

20. The area of the metal plate shown at the right, minus the hole area, is MOST NEARLY _____ square inches.
    A. 8.5
    B. 8.9
    C. 9.4
    D. 10.1

21. The percentage of the tank shown at the right that is filled with water is MOST NEARLY
    A. 33
    B. 35
    C. 37
    D. 39

22. Assume that a sump pit measures 10 feet long, 10 feet wide, and 12 feet deep. If each cubic foot of water is equal to 7.5 gallons, the amount of water in the sump when half full will be MOST NEARLY _____ gallons.

    A. 120   B. 1,200   C. 4,500   D. 9,000

23. If the water in a sump pit is 10 feet deep, the pressure at the bottom of the pit, in lbs. per sq. in., exerted by the water is MOST NEARLY (assuming water weighs 62.4 lbs./cu. ft.)

    A. 4.3   B. 52   C. 62.4   D. 624

24. If part of a walkway measuring 9 feet by 20 feet is to be replaced by concrete 6 inches thick, the cubic yards of concrete needed is MOST NEARLY

    A. 1 1/2   B. 3 1/2   C. 42   D. 90

25. A new bridge spanning a river is expected to carry 60,000 cars a day on a rainy day and 80,000 cars a day on other kinds of days.
If there is a $1 toll and one chance in four of a rainy day, the expected value of a day's revenue is

25.____

A. $35,000  B. $75,000  C. $95,000  D. $140,000

---

## KEY (CORRECT ANSWERS)

1. B
2. B
3. C
4. D
5. A

6. B
7. B
8. B
9. D
10. B

11. A
12. D
13. C
14. C
15. C

16. B
17. C
18. D
19. B
20. B

21. D
22. C
23. A
24. B
25. B

---

5 (#3)

# SOLUTIONS TO PROBLEMS

1. $4000 \div 33{,}000 \approx 12\%$
2. $(105)(.80) = 84$ tugboats
3. $140 - 45 - 52 - (2)(27) = -11$, so the shelf is overloaded by 11 lbs.
4. $3/8 = .375$
5. $(6'6\frac{1}{8}") \div 2 = 3'3\frac{1}{16}"$
6. Since 4 quarts = 1 gallon, 72 quarts = 18 gallons
7. 73 lbs. - 41 lbs. 3 oz. = 31 lbs. 13 oz.
8. $(\$153{,}696)(1.03) = \$158{,}307$
9. $(18{,}100 + 1{,}290 + 130 \times 1.10) = 21{,}472$ vehicles crossed the bridge on Friday.
10. 15 ft. 5 in. - 13 ft. 6 in. = 1 ft. 11 in.
11. Lane 1 had 1138 vehicles, whereas lane 2 had 1153 vehicles. Lane 1 had 15 fewer vehicles than lane 2.
12. Tolls collected = $\$1375.75 - \$230 = \$1145.75$. Then, $\$1145.75 \div \$1375.75 \approx 83\%$
13. $(134+210+213+234+111+118) \div 6 = 170$ vehicles
14. $21/28 = .75$ hr. Then, 1:50 PM - .75 hr. = 1:05 PM
15. Volume = $(15')(16')(10') = 2400$ cu.ft.
16. Cost = $(.21)(168)(1/4) = \$8.82$
17. $14{,}229 \div 17 = 837$
18. Total earnings = $(\$171.50)(15) = \$2572.50$
19. Total earnings = $\$24{,}500 + (1.10)(\$24{,}500) = \$51{,}450$
20. $(4)(3) - (\pi)(1)^2 = 8.9$ sq.in.
21. $\dfrac{7"}{18"} \approx 39\%$
22. Half the volume = $(1/2)(10)(10)(12) = 600$ cu.ft.
    Then, $(600)(7.5) = 4500$ gallons
23. Since 1728 cu.in. = 1 cu.ft., 62.4 lbs./cu.ft. = $0.36\overline{1}$ lbs./cu.in. With a depth of 10 ft. or 120 in., pressure = $(.0361 \times 120) \approx 4.3$ lbs./in.$^2$
24. $(9')(20')(1/2') = 90$ cu.ft. = $90/27 = 3\ 1/3$ or about $3\ 1/2$ cu.yds.
25. $(\$80{,}000)(.75) + (\$60{,}000)(.25) = \$75{,}000$

# SUPERVISION STUDY GUIDE

Social science has developed information about groups and leadership in general and supervisor-employee relationships in particular. Since organizational effectiveness is closely linked to the ability of supervisors to direct the activities of employees, these findings are important to executives everywhere.

IS A SUPERVISOR A LEADER?

First-line supervisors are found in all large business and government organizations. They are the men at the base of an organizational hierarchy. Decisions made by the head of the organization reach them through a network of intermediate positions. They are frequently referred to as part of the management team, but their duties seldom seem to support this description.

A supervisor of clerks, tax collectors, meat inspectors, or securities analysts is not charged with budget preparation. He cannot hire or fire the employees in his own unit on his say-so. He does not administer programs which require great planning, coordinating, or decision making.

Then what is he? He is the man who is directly in charge of a group of employees doing productive work for a business or government agency. If the work requires the use of machines, the men he supervises operate them. If the work requires the writing of reports, the men he supervises write them. He is expected to maintain a productive flow of work without creating problems which higher levels of management must solve. But is he a leader?

To carry out a specific part of an agency's mission, management creates a unit, staffs it with a group of employees and designates a supervisor to take charge of them. Management directs what this unit shall do, from time to time changes directions, and often indicates what the group should not do. Management presumably creates status for the supervisor by giving him more pay, a title, and special privileges.

Management asks a supervisor to get his workers to attain organizational goals, including the desired quantity and quality of production. Supposedly, he has authority to enable him to achieve this objective. Management at least assumes that by establishing the status of the supervisor's position, it has created sufficient authority to enable him to achieve these goals—not his goals, nor necessarily the group's, but management's goals.

In addition, supervision includes writing reports, keeping records of membership in a higher-level administrative group, industrial engineering, safety engineering, editorial duties, housekeeping duties, etc. The supervisor as a member of an organizational network, must be responsible to the changing demands of the management above him. At the same time, he must be responsive to the demands of the work group of which he is a member. He is placed in the difficult position of communicating and implementing new decisions, changed programs and revised production quotas for his work group, although he may have had little part in developing them.

It follows, then, that supervision has a special characteristic: achievement of goals, previously set by management, through the efforts of others. It is in this feature of the supervisor's job that we find the role of a leader in the sense of the following definition: *A leader is that person who most effectively influences group activities toward goal setting and goal achievements.*

This definition is broad. It covers both leaders in groups that come together voluntarily and in those brought together through a work assignment in a factory, store, or government agency. In the natural group, the authority necessary to attain goals is determined by the group membership and is granted by them. In the working group, it is apparent that the establishment of a supervisory position creates a predisposition on the part of employees to accept the authority of the occupant of that position. We cannot, however, assume that mere occupation confers authority sufficient to assure the accomplishment of an organization's goals.

Supervision is different, then, from leadership. The supervisor is expected to fulfill the role of leader but without obtaining a grant of authority from the group he supervises. The supervisor is expected to influence the group in the achieving of goals but is often handicapped by having little influence on the organizational process by which goals are set. The supervisor, because he works in an organizational setting, has the burdens of additional organizational duties and restrictions and requirements arising out of the fact that his position is subordinate to a hierarchy of higher-level supervisors. These differences between leadership and supervision are reflected in our definition: *Supervision is basically a leadership role, in a formal organization, which has as its objective the effective influencing of other employees.*

Even though these differences between supervision and leadership exist, a significant finding of experimenters in this field is that supervisors must be leaders to be successful.

The problem is: How can a supervisor exercise leadership in an organizational setting? We might say that the supervisor is expected to be a natural leader in a situation which does not come about naturally. His situation becomes really difficult in an organization which is more eager to make its supervisors into followers rather than leaders.

LEADERSHIP: NATURAL AND ORGANIZATIONAL

Leadership, in its usual sense of *natural* leadership, and supervision are not the same. In some cases, leadership embraces broader powers and functions than supervision; in other cases, supervision embraces more than leadership. This is true both because of the organization and technical aspects of the supervisor's job and because of the relatively freer setting and inherent authority of the natural leader.

The natural leader usually has much more authority and influence than the supervisor. Group members not only follow his command but prefer it that way. The employee, however, can appeal the supervisor's commands to his union or to the supervisor's superior or to the personnel office. These intercessors represent restrictions on the supervisor's power to lead.

The natural leader can gain greater membership involvement in the group's objectives, and he can change the objectives of the group. The supervisor can attempt to gain employee support only for management's objectives; he cannot set other objectives. In these instances leadership is broader than supervision.

The natural leader must depend upon whatever skills are available when seeking to attain objectives. The supervisor is trained in the administrative skills necessary to achieve management's goals. If he does not possess the requisite skills, however, he can call upon management's technicians.

A natural leader can maintain his leadership, in certain groups, merely by satisfying members' need for group affiliation. The supervisor must maintain his leadership by directing and organizing his group to achieve specific organizational goals set for him and his group by management. He must have a technical competence and a kind of coordinating ability which is not needed by many natural leaders.

A natural leader is responsible only to his group which grants him authority. The supervisor is responsible to management, which employs him, and also to the work group of which he is a member. The supervisor has the exceedingly difficult job of reconciling the demands of two groups frequently in conflict. He is often placed in the untenable position of trying to play two antagonistic roles. In the above instance, supervision is broader than leadership.

ORGANIZATIONAL INFLUENCES ON LEADERSHIP

The supervisor is both a product and a prisoner of the organization wherein we find him. The organization which creates the supervisor's position also obstructs, restricts, and channelizes the exercise of his duties. These influences extend beyond prescribed functional relationships to specific supervisory behavior. For example, even in a face-to-face situation involving one of his subordinates, the supervisor's actions are controlled to a great extent by his organization. His behavior must conform to the organization policy on human relations, rules which dictate personnel procedures, specific prohibitions governing conduct, the attitudes of his own superior, etc. He is not a free agent operating within the limits of his work group. His freedom of action is much more circumscribed than is generally admitted. The organizational influences which limit his leadership actions can be classified as structure, prescriptions, and proscriptions.

The organizational structure places each supervisor's position in context with other designated positions. It determines the relationships between his position and specific positions which impinge on his. The structure of the organization designates a certain position to which he looks for orders and information about his work. It gives a particular status to his position within a pattern of statuses from which he perceives that (1) certain positions are on a par, organizationally, with his, (2) other positions are subordinate, and (3) still others are superior.

The organizational structure determines those positions to which he should look for advice and assistance, and those positions to which he should give advice and assistance.

For instance, the organizational structure has predetermined that the supervisor of a clerical processing unit shall report to a supervisory position in a higher echelon. He shall have certain relationships with the supervisors of the work units which transmit work to and receive work from his unit. He shall discuss changes and clarification of procedures with certain staff units, such as organization and methods, cost accounting, and personnel. He shall consult supervisors of units which provide or receive special work assignments.

The organizational structure, however, establishes patterns other than those of the relationships of positions. These are the patterns of responsibility, authority, and expectations.

The supervisor is responsible for certain activities or results; he is presumably invested with the authority to achieve these. His set of authority and responsibility is interwoven with other sets to the end that all goals and functions of the organization are parceled out in small, manageable lots. This, of course, establishes a series of expectations: a single supervisor can perform his particular set of duties only upon the assumption that preceding or contiguous sets of duties have been, or are being carried out. At the same time, he is aware of the expectations of others that he will fulfill his functional role.

The structure of an organization establishes relationships between specified positions and specific expectations for these positions. The fact that these relationships and expectations are established is one thing; whether or not they are met is another.

PRESCRIPTIONS AND PROSCRIPTIONS

But let us return to the organizational influences which act to restrict the supervisor's exercise of leadership. These are the prescriptions and proscriptions generally in effect in all organizations, and those peculiar to a single organization. In brief these are the *thou shalt's* and the *thou shalt not's*.

Organizations not only prescribe certain duties for individual supervisory positions, they also prescribe specific methods and means of carrying out these duties and maintaining management-employee relations. These include rules, regulations, policy, and tradition. It does no good for the supervisor to say, *This seems to be the best way to handle such-and-such,* if the organization has established a routine for dealing with problems. For good or bad, there are rules that state that firings shall be executed in such a manner, accompanied by a certain notification; that training shall be conducted, and in this manner. Proscriptions are merely negative prescriptions; you may not discriminate against any employee because of politics or race; you shall not suspend any employee without following certain procedures and obtaining certain approvals.

Most of these prohibitions and rules apply to the area of interpersonal relations, precisely the area which is now arousing most interest on the part of administrators and managers. We have become concerned about the contrast between formally prescribed relationships and interpersonal relationships, and this brings us to the often discussed informal organization.

FORMAL AND INFORMAL ORGANIZATIONS

As we well know, the functions and activities of any organization are broken down into individual units of work called positions. Administrators must establish a pattern which will link these positions to each other and relate them to a system of authority and responsibility. Man-to-man are spelled out as plainly as possible for all to understand. Managers, then, build an official structure which we call the formal organization.

In these same organizations, employees react individually and in groups to institutionally determined roles. John, a worker, rides in the same carpool as Joe, a foreman. An unplanned communication develops. Harry, a machinist knows more about high-speed machining than his foreman or anyone else in his shop. An unofficial tool boss comes into being. Mary, who fought with Jane, is promoted over her. Jane now gives Mary's directions. A planned relationship fails to develop. The employees have built a structure which we call the informal organization.

*Formal organization is a system of management-prescribed relations between positions in an organization.*

*Informal organization is a network of unofficial relations between people in an organization.*

These definitions might lead us to the absurd conclusion that positions carry out formal activities and that employe4es spend their time in unofficial activities. We must recognize that organizational activities are in all cases carried out by people. The formal structure provides a needed framework within which interpersonal relations occur. What we call informal organization is the complex of normal, natural relations among employees. These personal relationships may be negative or positive. That is, they may impede or aid the achievement of organizational goals. For example, friendship between two supervisors greatly increases the probability of good cooperation and coordination between their sections. On the other hand, *buck passing* nullifies the formal structure by failure to meet a prescribed and expected responsibility.

It is improbable that an ideal organization exists where all activities are carried out in strict conformity to a formally prescribed pattern of functional roles. Informal organization arises because of the incompleteness and ambiguities in the network of formally prescribed relationships, or in response to the needs or inadequacies of supervisors or managers who hold prescribed functional roles in an organization. Many of these relationships are not prescribed by the organizational pattern; many cannot be prescribed; many should not be prescribed.

Management faces the problem of keeping the informal organization in harmony with the mission of the agency. One way to do this is to make sure that all employees have a clear understanding of and are sympathetic with that mission. The issuance of organizational charts, procedural manuals, and functional descriptions of the work to be done by divisions and sections helps communicate management's plans and goals. Issuances alone, of course, cannot do the whole job. They should be accompanied by oral discussion and explanation. Management must ensure that there is mutual understanding and acceptance of charts and procedures. More important is that management acquaint itself with the attitudes, activities, and peculiar brands of logic which govern the informal organization. Only through this type of knowledge can they and supervisors keep informal goals consistent with the agency mission.

## SUPERVISION STATUS AND FUNCTIONAL ROLE

A well-established supervisor is respected by the employees who work with him. They defer to his wishes. It is clear that a superior-subordinate relationship has been established. That is, status of the supervisor has been established in relation to other employees of the same work group. This same supervisor gains the respect of employees when he behaves in as certain manner. He will be expected, generally, to follow the customs of the group in such matters as dress, recreation, and manner of speaking. The group has a set of expectations as to his behavior. His position is a functional role which carries with it a collection of rights and obligations.

The position of supervisor usually has a status distinct from the individual who occupies it: it is much like a position description which exists whether or not there is an incumbent. The status of a supervisory position is valued higher than that of an employee position both because of the functional role of leadership which is assigned to it and because of the status symbols of titles, rights, and privileges which go with it.

Social ranking, or status, is not simple because it involves both the position and the man. An individual may be ranked higher than others because of his education, social background, perceived leadership ability, or conformity to group customs and ideals. If such a man is ranked higher by the members of a work group than their supervisor, the supervisor's effectiveness may be seriously undermined.

If the organization does not build and reinforce a supervisor's status, his position can be undermined in a different way. This will happen when managers go around rather than through the supervisor or designate him as a straw boss, acting boss, or otherwise not a real boss.

Let us clarify this last point. A role, and corresponding status, establishes a set of expectations. Employees expect their supervisor to do certain things and to act in certain ways. They are prepared to respond to that expected behavior. When the supervisor's behavior does not conform to their expectations, they are surprised, confused, and ill-at-ease. It becomes necessary for them to resolve their confusion, if they can. They might do this by turning to one of their own members for leadership. If the confusion continues, or their attempted solutions are not satisfactory, they will probably become a poorly motivated, non-cohesive group which cannot function very well.

## COMMUNICATION AND THE SUPERVISOR

In a recent survey, railroad workers reported that they rarely look to their supervisor for information about the company. This is startling, at least to us, because we ordinarily think of the supervisor as the link between management and worker. We expect the supervisor to be the prime source of information about the company. Actually, the railroad workers listed the supervisor next to last in the o5rder of their sources of information. Most surprising of all, the supervisors, themselves, stated that rumor and unofficial contacts were their principal sources of information. Here we see one of the reasons why supervisors may not be as effective as management desires.

The supervisor is not only being bypassed by his work group, he is being ignored, and his position weakened, by the very organization which is holding him responsible for the activities of his workers. If he is management's representative to the employee, then management has an obligation to keep him informed of its activities. This is necessary if he is to carry out his functions efficiently and maintain his leadership in the work group. The supervisor is expected to be a source of information; when he is not, his status is not clear, and employees are dissatisfied because he has not lived up to expectations.

By providing information to the supervisor to pass along to employees, we can strengthen his position as leader of the group, and increase satisfaction and cohesion within the group. Because he has more information than the other members, receives information sooner, and passes it along at the proper times, members turn to him as a source and also provide him with information in the hope of receiving some in return. From this, we can see an increase in group cohesiveness because:

- Employees are bound closer to their supervisor because he is *in the know*.
- There is less need to go outside the group for answers
- Employees will more quickly turn to the supervisor for enlightenment

The fact that he has the answers will also enhance the supervisor's standing in the eyes of his men. This increased status will serve to bolster his authority and control of the group and will probably result in improved morale and productivity.

The foregoing, of course, does not mean that all management information should be given out. There are obviously certain policy determinations and discussions which need not or cannot be transmitted to all supervisors. However, the supervisor must be kept as fully informed as possible so that he can answer questions when asked and can allay needless fears and anxieties. Further, the supervisor has the responsibility of encouraging employee questions and submissions of information. He must be able to present information to employees so that it is clearly understood and accepted. His attitude and manner should make it clear that he believes in what he is saying, that the information is necessary or desirable to the group, and that he is prepared to act on the basis of the information.

## SUPERVISION AND JOB PERFORMANCE

The productivity of work groups is a product; employees' efforts are multiplied by the supervision they receive. Many investigators have analyzed this relationship and have discovered elements of supervision which differentiate high and low production groups. These researchers have identified certain types of supervisory practices which they classify as *employee-centered* and other types which they classify as *production centered*.

The difference between these two kinds of supervision lies not in specific practices but in the approach or orientation to supervision. The employee-centered supervisor directs most of his efforts toward increasing employee motivation. He is concerned more with realizing the potential energy of persons than with administrative and technological methods of increasing efficiency and productivity. He is the man who finds ways of causing employees to want to work harder with the same tools. These supervisors emphasize the personal relations between their employees and themselves.

Now, obviously, these pictures are overdrawn. No one supervisor has all the virtues of the ideal type of employee-centered supervisor. And, fortunately, no one supervisor has all the bad traits found in many production-centered supervisors. We should remember that the various practices that researchers have fond which distinguish these two kinds of supervision represent the many practices and methods of supervisors of all gradations between these extremes. We should be careful, too, of the implications of the labels attached to the two types. For instance, being production-centered is not necessarily bad, since the principal responsibility of any supervisor is maintaining the production level that is expected of his work group. Being employee-centered may not necessarily be good, if the only result is a happy, chuckling crew of loafers. To return to the researchers' findings, employee-centered supervisors:

- Recommend promotions, transfers, pay increases
- Inform men about what is happening in the company
- Keep men posted on how well they are doing
- Hear complaints and grievances sympathetically
- Speak up for subordinates

Production-centered supervisors, on the other hand, don't do those things. They check on employees more frequently, give more detailed and frequent instructions, don't give reasons for changes, and are more punitive when mistakes are made. Employee-centered supervisors were reported to contribute to high morale and high production, whereas production-centered supervision was associated with lower morale and less production.

More recent findings, however, show that the relationship between supervision and productivity is not this simple. Investigators now report that high production is more frequently associated with supervisory practices which combine employee-centered behavior with concern for production. (This concern is not the same, however, as anxiety about production, which is the hallmark of our production-centered supervisor.) Let us examine these apparently contradictory findings and the premises from which they are derived.

SUPERVISION AND MORALE

Why do supervisory activities cause high or low production? As the name implies, the activities of the employee-centered supervisor tend to relate him more closely and satisfactorily to his workers. The production-centered supervisor's practices tend to separate him from his group and to foster antagonism. An analysis of this difference may answer our question.

Earlier, we pointed out that the supervisor is a type of leader and that leadership is intimately related to the group in which it occurs We discover, now, that an employee-centered supervisor's primary activities are concerned with both his leadership and his group membership. Such a supervisor is a member of a group and occupies a leadership role in that group.

These facts are sometimes obscured when we speak of the supervisor as management's representative, or as the organizational link between management and the employee, or as the end of the chain of command. If we really want to understand what it is we expect of the supervisor, we must remember that he is the designated leader of a group of employees to whom he is bound by interaction and interdependence.

Most of his actions are aimed, consciously or unconsciously, at strengthening membership ties in the group. This includes both making members more conscious that he is a member of their group) and causing members to identify themselves more closely with the group. These ends are accomplished by:

- making the group more attractive to the worker: they find satisfaction of their needs for recognition, friendship, enjoyable work, etc.;
- maintaining open communication: employees can express their views and obtain information about the organization
- giving assistance: members can seek advice on personal problems as well as their work; and
- acting as a buffer between the group and management: he speaks up for his men and explains the reasons for management's decisions.

Such actions both strengthen group cohesiveness and solidarity and affirm the supervisor's leadership position in the group.

DEFINING MORALE

This brings us back to a point mentioned earlier. We had said that employee-centered supervisors contribute to high morale as well as to high production. But how can we explain units which have low morale and high productivity, or vice versa? Usually production and morale are considered separately, partly because they are measured against different criteria and partly because, in some instances, they seem to be independent of each other.

Some of this difficulty may stem from confusion over definitions of morale. Morale has been defined as, or measured by, absences from work, satisfaction with job or company, dissension among members of work groups, productivity, apathy or lack of interest, readiness to help others, and a general aura of happiness as rated by observers. Some of these criteria of morale are not subject to the influence of the supervisor, and some of them are not clearly related to productivity. Definitions like these invite findings of low morale coupled with high production.

Both productivity and morale can be influenced by environmental factors not under the control of group members or supervisors. Such things as plant layout, organizational structure and goals, lighting, ventilation, communications, and management planning may have an adverse or desirable effect.

We might resolve the dilemma by defining morale on the basis of our understanding of the supervisor as leader of a group; morale is the degree of satisfaction of group members with their leadership. In this light, the supervisor's employee-centered activities bear a clear relation to morale. His efforts to increase employee identification with the group and to strengthen his leadership lead to greater satisfaction with that leadership. By increasing group cohesiveness and by demonstrating that his influence and power can aid the group, he is able to enhance his leadership status and afford satisfaction to the group.

SUPERVISION, PRODUCTION, AND MORALE

There are factors within the organization itself which determine whether increased production is possible:

- Are production goals expressed in terms understandable to employees and are they realistic?
- Do supervisors responsible for production respect the agency mission and production goals?
- If employees do not know how to do the job well, does management provide a trainer—often the supervisor—who can teach efficient work methods?

There are other factors within the work group which determine whether increased production will be attained:

- Is leadership present which can bring about the desired level of production?
- Are production goals accepted by employees as reasonable and attainable?
- If group effort is involved, are members able to coordinate their efforts?

Research findings confirm the view that an employee-centered supervisor can achieve higher morale than a production-centered supervisor. Managers may well ask what is the relationship between this and production.

Supervision is production-oriented to the extent that it focuses attention on achieving organizational goals, and plans and devises methods for attaining them; it is employee-centered to the extent that it focuses attention on employee attitudes toward those goals, and plans and works toward maintenance of employee satisfaction.

High productivity and low morale result when a supervisor plans and organizes work efficiently but cannot achieve high membership satisfaction. Low production and high morale result when a supervisor, though keeping members satisfied with his leadership, either has not gained acceptance of organizational goals or does not have the technical competence to achieve them.

The relationship between supervision, morale, and productivity is an interdependent one, with the supervisor playing an integral role due to his ability to influence productivity and morale independently of each other.

A supervisor who can plan his work well has good technical knowledge, and who can install better production methods can raise production without necessarily increasing group satisfaction. On the other hand, a supervisor who can motivate his employees and keep them satisfied with his leadership can gain high production in spite of technical difficulties and environmental obstacles.

CLIMATE AND SUPERVISION

Climate, the intangible environment of an organization made up of attitudes, beliefs, and traditions, plays a large part in morale, productivity, and supervision. Usually when we speak of climate and its relationship to morale and productivity, we talk about the merits of *democratic* versus *authoritarian* climate. Employees seem to produce more and have higher morale in a democratic climate, whereas in an authoritarian climate, the reverse seems to be true or so the researchers tell us. We would do well to determine what these terms mean to supervision.

Perhaps most of our difficulty in understanding and applying these concepts comes from our emotional reactions to the words themselves. For example, authoritarian climate is usually painted as the very blackest kind of dictatorship. This is not surprising, because we are usually expected to believe that it is invariably bad. Conversely, democratic climate is drawn to make the driven snow look impure by comparison.

Now these descriptions are most probably true when we talk about our political processes, or town meetings, or freedom of speech. However, the same labels have been used by social scientists in other contexts and have also been applied to government and business organizations, without it, it seems, any recognition that the meanings and their social values may have changed somewhat

For example, these labels were used in experiments conducted in an informal classroom setting using 11-year-old boys as subjects. The descriptive labels applied to the climate of the setting as well as the type of leadership practiced. When these labels were transferred to a management setting, it seems that many presumed that they principally meant the king of leadership rather than climate. We can see that there is a great difference between the experimental and management settings and that leadership practices for one might be inappropriate for the other.

It is doubtful that formal work organizations can be anything but authoritarian, in that goals are set by management and a hierarchy exists through which decisions and orders from the top are transmitted downward. Organizations are authoritarian by structure and need; direction and control are placed in the hands of a few in order to gain fast and efficient decision making. Now this does not mean to describe a dictatorship. It is merely the recognition of the fact that direction of organizational affairs comes from above. It should be noted that leadership in some natural groups is, in this sense, authoritarian.

Granting that formal organizations have this kind of authoritarian leadership, can there be a democratic climate? Certainly there can be, but we would want to define and delimit this term. A more realistic meaning of democratic climate in organizations is the use of permissive and participatory methods in management-employee relations. That is, a mutual exchange of information and explanation with the granting of individual freedom within certain restricted and defined limits. However, it is not our purpose to debate the merits of authoritarianism versus democracy. We recognize that within the small work group there is a need for freedom from constraint and an increase in participation in order to achieve organizational goals within the framework of the organizational movement.

Another aspect of climate is best expressed by this familiar, and true, saying: actions speak louder than words. Of particular concern to us is this effect of management climate on the behavior of supervisors, particularly in employee-centered activities.

There have been reports of disappointment with efforts to make supervisors ore employee-centered. Managers state that, since research has shown ways of improving human relations, supervisors should begin to practice these methods. Usually a training course in human relations is established; and supervisors are given this training. Managers then sit back and wait for the expected improvements, only to find that there are none.

If we wish to produce changes in the supervisor's behavior, the climate must be made appropriate and rewarding to the changed behavior. This means that top-level attitudes and behavior cannot deny or contradict the change we are attempting to effect. Basic changes in organizational behavior cannot be made with any permanence, unless we provide an environment that is receptive to the changes and rewards those persons who do change.

IMPROVING SUPERVISION

Anyone who has read this far might expect to find *A Dozen Rules for Dealing With Employees* or *29 Steps to Supervisory Success*. We will not provide such a list.

Simple rules suffer from their simplicity. They ignore the complexities of human behavior. Reliance upon rules may cause supervisors to concentrate on superficial aspects of their relations with employees. It may preclude genuine understanding.

The supervisor who relies on a list of rules tends to think of people in mechanistic terms. In a certain situation, he uses *Rule No. 3*. Employees are not treated as thinking and feeling persons, but rather as figures in a formula: Rule 3 applied to employee X = Production.

Employees usually recognize mechanical manipulation and become dissatisfied and resentful. They lose faith in, and respect for, their supervisor, and this may be reflected in lower morale and productivity.

We do not mean that supervisors must become social science experts if they wish to improve. Reports of current research indicate that there are two major parts of their job which can be strengthened through self-improvement: (1) Work planning, including technical skills, and (2) motivation of employees.

The most effective supervisors combine excellence in the administrative and technical aspects of their work with friendly and considerate personal relations with their employees.

## CRITICAL PERSONAL RELATIONS

Later in this chapter we shall talk about administrative aspects of supervision, but first let us comment on *friendly and considerate personal relations*. We have discussed this subject throughout the preceding chapters, but we want to review some of the critical supervisory influences on personal relations.

Closeness of Supervision: The closeness of supervision has an important effect on productivity and morale. Mann and Dent found that supervisors of low-producing units supervise very closely, while high-producing supervisors exercise only general supervision. It was found that the low-producing supervisors:

- check on employees more frequently
- give more detailed and frequent instructions
- limit employee's freedom to do job in own way

Workers who felt less closely supervised reported that they were better satisfied with their jobs and the company. We should note that the manner or attitude of the supervisor has an important bearing on whether employees perceive supervision as being close or general.

These findings are another way of saying that supervision does not mean standing over the employee and telling him what to do and when and how to do it. The more effective supervisor tells his employees what is required, giving general instructions.

## COMMUNICATION

Supervisors of high-production units consider communication as one of the most important aspects of their job. Effective communication is used by these supervisors to achieve better interpersonal relations and improved employee motivation. Low-production supervisors do not rate communications as highly important.

High-producing supervisors find that an important aid to more effective communication is listening. They are ready to listen to both personal problems or interests and questions about the work. This does not mean that they are *nosey* or meddle in their employees' personal lives, but rather that they show a willingness to listen, and do listen, if their employees wish to discuss problems.

These supervisors inform employees about forthcoming changes in work; they discuss agency policy with employees; and they make sure that each employee knows how well he is doing. What these supervisors do is use two-way communication effectively. Unless the supervisor freely imparts information, he will not receive information in return.

Attitudes and perception are frequently affected by communication or the lack of it. Research surveys reveal that many supervisors are not aware of their employees' attitudes, nor do they know what personal reactions their supervision arouses. Through frank discussion with employees, they have been surprised to discover employee beliefs about which they were ignorant. Discussion sometimes reveals that the supervisor and his employees have totally different impressions about the same event. The supervisor should be constantly on the alert for misconceptions about his words and deeds. He must remember that, although his actions are perfectly clear to himself, they may be, and frequently are, viewed differently by employees.

Failure to communicate information results in misconceptions and false assumptions. What you say and how you say it will strongly affect your employees' attitudes and perceptions. By giving them available information, you can prevent misconceptions; by discussion, you may be able to change attitudes; by questioning, you can discover what the perceptions and assumptions really are. And it need hardly be added that actions should conform very closely to words.

If we were to attempt to reduce the above discussion on communication to rules, we would have a long list which would be based on one cardinal principle: Don't make assumptions!

- Don't assume that your employees know; tell them.
- Don't assume that you know how they feel; find out.
- Don't assume that they understand; clarify.

## 20 SUPERVISORY HINTS

1. Avoid inconsistency.
2. Always give employees a chance to explain their action before taking disciplinary action. Don't allow too much time for a "cooling off" period before disciplining an employee.
3. Be specific in your criticisms.
4. Delegate responsibility wisely.
5. Do not argue or lose your temper, and avoid being impatient.
6. Promote mutual respect and be fair, impartial, and open-minded.
7. Keep in mind that asking for employees' advice and input can be helpful in decision making.
8. If you make promises, keep them.
9. Always keep the feelings, abilities, dignity and motives of your staff in mind.
10. Remain loyal to your employees' interests.
11. Never criticize employees in front of others, or treat employees like children.
12. Admit mistakes. Don't place blame on your employees, or make excuses.
13. Be reasonable in your expectations, give complete instructions, and establish well-planned goals.
14. Be knowledgeable about office details and procedures, but avoid becoming bogged down in details.
15. Avoid supervising too closely or too loosely. Employees should also view you as an approachable supervisor.
16. Remember that employees' personal problems may affect job performance, but become involved only when appropriate.
17. Work to develop workers, and to instill a feeling of cooperation while working toward mutual goals.
18. Do not overpraise or underpraise, be properly appreciative.
19. Never ask an employee to discipline someone for you.
20. A complaint, even if unjustified, should be taken seriously.

# NOTES

www.ingramcontent.com/pod-product-compliance
Lightning Source LLC
Chambersburg PA
CBHW080323020526

44117CB00035B/2637